OPERATING IN

THE 9 DIMENSIONS

OF

TONGUES

EMMANUEL MAKARIOS

DEDICATION

This book is dedicated to God, the Father,

the Son, and the Holy Spirit.

TABLE OF CONTENT

INTRODUCTION

Every believer ought to be head-over-heels in love with the Holy Spirit and His gift of speaking in tongues. The unknown tongue is a language of the Spirit. It is an empowerment that comes upon believers from the outpouring of the Holy Spirit. It is the promise of God for everyone who believes in Jesus Christ, the Messiah. The clog that causes the drawbacks in the heart of people about receiving the gift of speaking in tongues is centered on the unfruitful understanding in the place of prayer. The good news is that it is possible to desire the gift of interpretation of tongues for the edification of self and the church at large. When speaking in tongues is added to the gift of interpretation it becomes the gift of prophecy for edifying the church.

"And these signs shall follow them that believe; In my name shall they cast out devils; they shall speak with new tongues" (Mark 16:17 KJV).

Speaking in tongues is the gift of the Spirit that enables us to speak mysteries to God. Whenever we speak to God with this language, we speak at a very high amplitude of spiritual knowledge and divine sagacity.
"For he that speaketh in an unknown tongue speaketh not unto men, but unto God: for no man understandeth him; howbeit in the spirit he speaketh mysteries" (1 Corinthians 14:2 KJV).

Furthermore, this book outlines the dimensions of the unknown tongues and the general habitude of the natural tongues. Baptism of the Spirit, and many more will be discussed in this book. You will learn so much about diverse tongues. Be blessed as you read!

EMMANUEL MAKARIOS

Chapter

BREATH, SOUND, AND TONGUES

CHAPTER ONE
BREATH, SOUND, AND TONGUES

"Though I speak with the tongues of men and of angels, and have not charity, I am become as sounding brass, or a tinkling cymbal" (1 Corinthians 13:1 KJV).

In the kingdom of God, everything is well organized with structures and patterns. Everything created by God has sound encoded in it. God released a sound "let there be light" and there was light. God spoke everything forth one after the other, through the code of His breath. What is that? Sound! Everything emanated from God's sound. Everything exists in form of sound. Only sound can alter creation forms and patterns. Creation is sound code in shape. The tongues of men are sounds with meaning. God made everything in a way that it can communicate, including nature. What God made that cannot communicate is not necessarily in existence. In the spirit realm, everything created is seen as a spirit because God has encoded sound in them.

Each time I remember Adam, the first man created and his wife Eve, the question that does come to my heart is "what language did Adam use in naming animals and all that he named?" Seeing that the bible says

"So Adam gave names to all cattle, to the birds of the air, and to every beast of the field. But for Adam there was not found a helper comparable to him" (Genesis 2:20 KJV).

Since He was the first man to be created who taught Him the language? No one! Adam used the power and the revelation of breath. He opened his mouth and named them as the breath of deity gave him understanding: *"But there is a spirit in man, And the breath of the Almighty gives him understanding" (Job 32:8 KJV)*. Adam had no understanding of how things were supposed to be in the spirit or in the physical, however, the breath of the Lord gave him the understanding. Whatever Adam called everything around him is a function of the breath understanding given to him. The breath understanding is a code of the interpretation of tongues. The breath is an inspiration of God. Everything created is breath coded. It is contrived from the inspiration and divinity of God.

Paul wrote in the scripture equating speaking in tongues of either an angel or of man to making a sound. He said, *"though I speak with the tongues of men and of angels, and have not charity, I am become as sounding brass, or a tinkling cymbal" (1 Corinthians 13:1 KJV).*

According to Paul's writing, love can interpret sound in a zone of life, else the sound will be like that of an ordinary-sounding brass or tinkling cymbal. All tongues are sounds in every realm. The sound that creation makes has meaning in its realms.

"For all creation is waiting eagerly for that future day when God will reveal who his children really are. Against its will, all creation was subjected to God's curse. But with eager hope, the creation looks forward to the day when it will join God's children in glorious freedom from death and decay. For we know that all creation has been groaning as in the pains of childbirth right up to the present time. And we believers also groan, even though we have the Holy Spirit within us as a foretaste of future glory, for we long for our bodies to be released from sin and suffering. We, too, wait with eager hope for the day when God will give us our full rights as his adopted children, including the new bodies he has promised us. We were given this hope when we were saved. If we already have something, we don't need to hope for it"
(1 Corinthians 14:19-24 NLT).

How do you decode the tongue of creation? It is through the sounds they make. The breath is encoded in them. The Bible says creation is in pain and groaning right up to this present day. This implicit groaning is a shout for freedom. Who would have known that creation is crying for freedom from decay except through revelations? Every tongue is a sound. When the sound has no meaning, it is called gibberish. The gibberish of sound is only valid in the realm of ignorance.

"Now, brethren, if I come unto you speaking with tongues, what shall I profit you, except I shall speak to you either by revelation, or by knowledge, or by prophesying, or by doctrine? And even things without life giving sound, whether pipe or harp, except they give a distinction in the sounds, how shall it be known what is piped or harped? For if the trumpet gives an uncertain sound, who shall prepare himself to the battle? So likewise ye, except ye utter by the tongue words easy to be understood, how shall it be

known what is spoken? for ye shall speak into the air"
(1 Corinthians 14:6-9 KJV).

The only thing that can stop sound from being gibberish is knowledge and revelation. The moment knowledge confronts sounds, a well-defined tongue and interpretation is seen. There are four kinds of tongues. There is the tongue of men, the tongue of other creation, the angelic tongues, and the unknown tongues. This chapter is just an introduction, we shall discuss the four tongues one after the other later in this book.

The tongues created by God are for communication whether in Heaven or on earth. There are a few purposes of this communication; socialization among angels and spirits, adequate control, altering of wrong attitudes, motivation to carry out divine tasks, expression of interest, and releasing of vital information. These purposes are carried out among the living and the non-living.

Breath, Sound, And Tongues Transmutation

When there is homogeneity between sound, breath, and tongues a matter can be birthed. Matter is anything that has weight and occupies space according to the world of science. Such matter can either be spiritual or physical. The congruence of the above can cause things to either appear or disappear in the real world.

Every sound is coded with the breath, and for sound to be released from the mouth of humans, it must be through tongues. This is the principle the Lord taught Ezekiel:

"Thus saith the Lord God unto these bones; Behold, I will cause breath to enter into you, and ye shall live: And I will lay sinews upon you, and will bring up flesh upon you, and cover you with skin, and put breath in you, and ye shall live; and ye shall know that I am the Lord. So I prophesied as I was commanded: and as I prophesied, there was a noise, and behold a shaking, and the bones came together, bone to his bone" (Ezekiel 37:5-7 KJV).

Looking at the above scripture, we could see that breath and sound when released through tongues can create objects or matter. Alternatively, we can refer to prophecy as tongues in the above. Prying the same scripture further, you could see the amazing effect of the combination. When breath is released from the tongue expect a change.

The description of a word in motion is breath becoming sound through the tongue. When this happens life can be formed. This is the reason why we are looking at its transmutation. The Word of the Lord cannot be broken when it is released from His mouth, it is usually a compound element of sound breath and tongue transmuting into things in this horizon. The Lord Himself described the transmutation:

"For as the rain cometh down, and the snow from heaven, and returneth not thither, but watereth the earth, and maketh it brings forth and bud, that it may give seed to the sower, and bread to the eater: So shall my word be that goeth forth out of my mouth: it shall not return unto me void, but it shall accomplish that which I please, and it shall prosper in the thing whereto I sent it" (Isaiah 55:10-11 KJV).

Breath-sound whether it is silent, short, loud, or cryptic, is usually a great weapon for changing any situation. We can change everything in our world through this revelation.

"By the breath of God frost is given: and the breadth of the waters is straitened (Job 37:10 KJV).
"The spirit of God hath made me, and the breath of the Almighty hath given me life" (Job 33:4 KJV).
All life's issues can be straightened through breath.

Key Activation Prayers

Awesome Holy Spirit come upon me with your fresh power and anointing let the seal of this dimension be broken for the ease of my operation. Right now I declare that I am making use of the breath of the Holy Spirit. I take advantage of this power on a daily basis in Jesus' name. Amen!

Chapter

2

THE TWO KINDS OF TONGUE BOOKS AND TONGUE WRITINGS

CHAPTER TWO

THE TWO KINDS OF TONGUE BOOKS AND TONGUE WRITINGS

"And I saw the dead, small and great, stand before God; and the books were opened: and another book was opened, which is the book of life: and the dead were judged out of those things which were written in the books, according to their works." (Genesis Revelation 20:12 KJV).

Every civilization and ecosystem occupied by spirits and humans have names and writings existing for nomenclature, documentation, identification, and memorials. The spirit and human ecosystems have variations in civilizations, legislations, architecture, as well as the apprehension of life. Hence, a difference in interaction with the Godhead is birthed, leading to the two kinds of books and writings within the two ecosystems that will be discussed in this book. Thus, there are two kinds of primeval books and writings of the two civilizations;

1.   The Earthly-Tongue Books and the Earthly-Tongue Writing.
2.   The Heavenly-Tongue Books and The Heavenly-Tongue Writings.

God is the creator who made all things through His wisdom and His word. Creation found its existence in God *"Through faith we understand that the worlds were framed by the word of God, so that things which are seen were not made of things which do appear" (Hebrew 11:3 KJV)*. Without God, nothing can find existence. Let us look at the above-listed one after the other.

1.   The Earthly-Tongue Books and The Earthly-Tongue Writing

I. The Earthly-Tongue Books

A book is an essential material on earth. It is a bound set of blank sheets for writing. On the horizon called earth, everything is advanced by man after the narrative in the book of Genesis 1. Of course, with the help of God, Man began to document his thoughts, findings, feelings, and the nomenclature of creation. With more demands rising for history and memorials on the earth, humans matured earthly writings and books intending to communicate across time and space. Men want to carry memorials with them as they traded, migrated, and conquered the territories given to them by God. Although from inception, including the generation of Adam, the first usages of writings and books are for a census, general counting, and nomenclature. Men also held in their minds the idea to communicate beyond the grave and death. Hence, writings and books were used to express the insatiable desires of men.

In addition, the earthly kind of book has many types of forms. There are many things that have the resemblance of a book. Some are tablets of stone, computers, and other forms. The ancient book form called the codex was part of the first to be created by the Romans around the second to third Century. It was made in a way that sheets of papyrus, parchment, or paper would be folded in half and sewn jointly at the fold.

"The cloke that I left at Troas with Carpus, when thou comest, bring with thee, and the books, but especially the parchments" (2 Timothy 4:13KJV).

As a reader in that age, you would have to open the pages to show the two columns of text sharing a page. The codex was formed to replace the scrolls. The codex was a bound stack of hand-written sheets only on one side. Although, there were accesses granted to individual and independent pages through well-defined isolations.

The Bible is a collection of books. It is a unique and profound book that has shaped culture, laws, and faith throughout many generations. It is written under supernatural guidance by Holy men as inspired by the Holy Spirit. It is an ancient writing that contains sixty-six books (thirty-nine in Old Testament, twenty-seven in New Testament) and fourteen in Apocrypha. There are a few other books mentioned in the Bible. Take a look at the list below:

The Book of the Generation of Adam

The book was written to keep the record of the names of the people in the generation of Adam: *"This is the book of the generations of Adam. In the day that God created man, in the likeness of God made he him" (Genesis 5:1).* It was written in order keep a memorial of what happened to the people in the first order of creation. Nothing again could be discussed in this book other than the things and names having to do with the generation of Adam.

The Book of the Law

This is the same as the book of the covenant. It is the book of the commandments of God. It was the decree of God for the Old Testament. The scripture says *"As Moses the servant of the Lord commanded the children of Israel, as it is written in the book of the law of Moses, an altar of whole stones, over which no man hath lift up any iron: and they offered thereon burnt*

offerings unto the Lord, and sacrificed peace offerings" (Joshua 8:31).
"And he took the book of the covenant, and read in the audience of the people: and they said, All that the Lord hath said will we do, and be obedient" (Exodus 24:7).

The Book of the Lamb and the Book of Life

This is the book with the details of everyone that got born again in Christ through the washing of the blood: The scripture says *"And it was given unto him to make war with the saints, and to overcome them: and power was given him over all kindreds, and tongues, and nations and all that dwell upon the earth shall worship him, whose names are not written in the book of life of the Lamb slain from the foundation of the world"* (Revelations 13:8 KJV). The book is a book of righteous people:

"And I saw the dead, small and great, stand before God; and the books were opened: and another book was opened, which is the book of life: and the dead were judged out of those things which were written in the books, according to their works (Revelations 20:12).

"Yet now, if thou wilt forgive their sin--; and if not, blot me, I pray thee, out of thy book which thou hast written. And the Lord said unto Moses, whosoever hath sinned against me, him will I blot out of my book" (Exodus 32:32-33).
"Notwithstanding in this rejoice not, that the spirits are subject unto you; but rather rejoice, because your names are written in heaven" (Luke 10:20).
Let them be blotted out of the book of the living, and not be written with the righteous (Psalms 69:28).

The Book of the Wars of the Lord

This is the book that retains the exceptional attributes of God specially for fighting for His people in different times and seasons. A good example is how God fought for the Israelites at the red sea where Moses said, "stand still and see the salvation of your God". What He did for them on that day was called the War of the Lord:
"Wherefore it is said in the book of the wars of the Lord, what he did in the Red Sea, and in the brooks of Arnon" (Numbers 21:14).

The Book of Jasher

The book of Jasher recorded some accounts of wars in the Bible. Exceptional skills of war and victories were recorded in this book for a memorial. Some of the accounts recorded there are also detailed in some specific chapters of the bible. It is the testimony of God concerning how He used many of His mighty men in different places and at different times:

> *"And the sun stood still, and the moon stayed, until the people had avenged themselves upon their enemies. Is not this written in the book of Jasher? So the sun stood still in the midst of heaven, and hasted not to go down about a whole day" (Joshua 10:13).*
> *"Also, he bade them teach the children of Judah the use of the bow: behold, it is written in the book of Jasher" (2 Samuel 1:18).*

The Book of the Acts of Solomon

The book of the acts of Solomon is different from the book of the songs of Solomon or Ecclesiastes. The book is also written to keep the record of Solomon's dealing while he was on the earth: "And the rest of the acts of Solomon, and all that he did, and his wisdom, are they not written in the book of the acts of Solomon?" (1 kings 11:41).

The Book of the Chronicles of the Kings of Israel and Judah

So many people particularly kings who walked with God reigned on the earth and personally did remarkable things here on earth had their names written in some other books like this for proper documentation of history that will serve as deterrence for other kings: *"And the rest of the acts of Jeroboam, how he warred, and how he reigned, behold, they are written in the book of the chronicles of the kings of Israel"* (1 kings 14:19).

> *"Now the rest of the acts of Nadab, and all that he did, are they not written in the book of the chronicles of the kings of Israel?" (1 kings 15:31).*
> *Now the rest of the acts of Rehoboam, and all that he did, are they not written in the book of the chronicles of the kings of Judah? (1 kings 14:29).*
> *"Now the rest of the acts of Abijam, and all that he did, are they not written in the book of the chronicles of the kings of Judah? And there was war between Abijam and Jeroboam" 1 king 15:7).*
> *"Now the rest of the acts of Jehoshaphat, and his might that he shewed, and how he warred,are they not written in the book of the chronicles of the kings of Judah?" (1 kings 22:45).*

The Book of Nathan the Prophet

Nathan was one of the prophets who walked with David. On the account of his walk with God, he wrote a book. This book kept the details of God's word and instructions to him concerning the kings of his days *"Now the acts of David the king, first and last, behold, they are written in the book of Samuel the seer, and in the book of Nathan the prophet, and in the book of Gad the seer" (1 Chronicles 29:29).*

"Now the rest of the acts of Solomon, first and last, are they not written in the book of Nathan the prophet, and in the prophecy of Ahijah the Shilonite, and in the visions of Iddo the seer against Jeroboam the son of Nebat?" (2 Chronicles 9:29).

The Book of Gad the Seer

Gad was also a prominent seer in his time. He wrote books. He kept the memorial of instructions and everything that the Lord said to him: *"Now the acts of David the king, first and last, behold, they are written in the book of Samuel the seer, and in the book of Nathan the prophet, and in the book of Gad the seer" (1 Chronicles 29:29).*

The Book of Shemaiah the Prophet

Shemaiah was also a prominent prophet. One thing I observe about the prophets in those days is their ability to write: *"Now the acts of Rehoboam, first and last, are they not written in the book of Shemaiah the prophet, and of Iddo the seer concerning genealogies? And there were wars between Rehoboam and Jeroboam continually" (2 Chronicles 12:15).*

The Book of Iddo the Seer

The seer Iddo was also a very prolific writer. He wrote certain memorials about his days: *"Now the acts of Rehoboam, first and last, are they not written in the book of Shemaiah the prophet, and of Iddo the seer concerning genealogies? And there were wars between Rehoboam and Jeroboam continually" (2 Chronicles 12:15).*

The Book of Jehu the Son of Hanani

Jehu was also not left out of the experience, He also wrote a book: *"Now the rest of the acts of Jehoshaphat, first and last, behold, they are written in the book of Jehu the son of Hanani, who is mentioned in the book of the kings of Israel" (2 Chronicles 20:34).*

These were some of the books mentioned in the Bible. They were all written for a memorial! The books were used to pass on instructions from one age to another. Values were preserved beyond death. Secrets were also retained through them.

The holy men in the early Bible days used their knowledge of the earthly code of writing to preserve the secrets of God. The prophets, apostles, teachers, evangelists, and pastors retained the values and passed them through books to the next generations. They came to the world to fulfill God's purpose through, the understanding of their role from the books written for memorials on earth.

> *"Then said I, Lo, I come in the volume of the book it is written of me to do thy will, O God" (Hebrew 10:7).*

Jesus the son of God understood His role on earth through the volume of books. Purposes, destinies, and divine secrets are preserved through the wisdom code of books. God has designed it that way. Below are a few purposes of the earthly books:

1. Sharing of information.
2. Preserving secrets.
3. Passing stories to the next generation.
4. Preserving genealogical order.
5. Preserving information about the creation.
6. Archiving history.
7. Communicating values across time and space.
8. Preserving generational assets.
9. Educating the people.
10. Communicating the mind of God on the earth.

ii The Earthly-Tongue Writing

Earthly Tongue writings were mostly inscriptions of ink, fire, or some evident spiritual impact on physical objects. God uses writings to preserve His purposes on earth. It is these writings that culminate in scrolls and books.

"And the Lord said unto Moses, write this for a memorial in a book, and rehearse it in the ears of Joshua: for I will utterly put out the remembrance of Amalek from under heaven" (Exodus 17:14 KJV).

The idiosyncrasy of writing generally can be some voices, ideas, presentations, conventions, organizations, word choices, letters, and instruction fluency. This idiosyncrasy can be expressed in form of a narrative, descriptive, persuasive, and expository methodology. An example of a persuasive writing is the book of *1 John 5: 13 which says… "These things have I written unto you that believe on the name of the Son of God; that ye may know that ye have eternal life, and that ye may believe on the name of the Son of God".*

Most messages from God were recorded through earthly writing. Many prophets and Apostles were instructed to write down instructions from Him. They were told to pass His mind from one generation to the next through writing:

"This shall be written for the generation to come: and the people which shall be created shall praise the Lord" (Psalm 102:18 KJV).

The above scripture adumbrates the mind of God in preserving many generations. God loves writing. He believes in writing. He instituted writing. No matter how vast the race of God's people might be on the earth, God can reach out to them through writing. Writing is the voice of God.

Paul through the awareness of how God preserves said *"Do we begin again to commend ourselves? Or need we, as some others, epistles of commendation to you, or letters of commendation from you?" (2 Corinthians 3:1 KJV)*, because those letters were the things that became epistles and some of the scriptures today. Earthly writing is inspired by God for communicating, revealing, and preserving order and secrets:

"And he gave unto Moses, when he had made an end of communing with him upon mount Sinai, two tables of testimony, tables of stone, written with the finger of God" (Exodus 31:18 KJV).

Let's compare what Job said in the two versions of the Bible below… *"Oh, that my words were recorded, that they were written on a scroll, that they were inscribed with an iron tool on lead, or engraved in rock forever!"* (Job 19:23-24 NIV), and… *"Oh that my words were now written! Oh that they were printed in a book! That they were graven with an iron pen and lead in the rock forever!"* (Job 19:23-24 KJV).

Our words are writing. The writing of our words is the writing of the tongue. The expression of Job above will cause us to be apt in bringing perspective to the earthly writings from history. To mention a few, in my opinion, tongue writing, fire writing, Ink writing, and Hard Pen writing, give us an idea of various tools of writing from the ancient world. The examples are well highlighted below: The Egyptian reed Pen; it is a small reed pen sharpened to a point and used to draw hieroglyphs on clay tablets or sometimes used in ink to draw on papyrus. In ancient times, the Romans devised the Roman metal pen for writing. This metal writing instrument is what gave birth to the modern-day metal pen.

Moreover, in the middle age, the quill was introduced as a large feather with a hollow, sharpened to a point and dipped in ink to write. Although, there was the advent of the cane pen most used from antiquity in the middle age to write on parchment and papyrus and still exists in Arabic calligraphy till date. Also, the pointed instrument which is used for etching wax tablets by the ancient is called a stylus. Besides these, there are steel pens and lead pencils. The former is a curved point instrument horsed on a handle. It is usually dipped in the inkwell to write. The Latter on the contrary is a decorative-end lead pencil used from antiquity in the middle age and later replaced with graphite lead pencil. The pertinent writing tools were used by different ministers to write the mind of God and pass it on from one generation to the other.

The above tools of writing were the aids that succored communication beyond space, time, and one generation as men began to sense the need to preserve values and information. Do not undermine the power of God to instruct the mind to preserve a generation.

The tongue is a powerful tool for writing. Through the tongue, Adam named creation. Through the tongue of man, life is named and everything secured relevance. We have to be careful with our tongue because the tongue is a pen.

"Even so the tongue is a little member, and boasteth great things. Behold, how great a matter a little fire kindleth! And the tongue is a fire, a world of iniquity: so is the tongue among our members, that it defileth the whole body, and setteth on fire the course of nature; and it is set on fire of hell. For every kind of beasts, and of birds, and of serpents, and of things in the sea, is tamed, and hath been tamed of mankind: But the tongue can no man tame; it is an unruly evil, full of deadly poison" (James 3:5-8 KJV).

Name-calling is a form of writing. A confession is a form of writing on nature. Adam's experience is a picture of what writing on nature looks like.

"And out of the ground the Lord God formed every beast of the field, and every fowl of the air; and brought them unto Adam to see what he would call them: and whatsoever Adam called every living creature, that was the name thereof" (Genesis 2:19 KJV).

Man's tongue is a writing tool. It writes about life and nature. Nature takes only the shape of whatever man's tongue writes on it.

"My heart is inditing a good matter: I speak of the things which I have made touching the king: my tongue is the pen of a ready writer" (Psalm 45:1 KJV). Again, the tongue of man is a pen always waiting and ready to write something.

2.   Heavenly Tongue Books and The Heavenly Tongue Writing
i. The Heavenly-Tongue Books

In heaven there are books. These books are either written by God or angels. When searching for books in Heaven, they exist in heaven in different forms as scrolls and books; spiritual papers, parchment, scriptures, and manuscripts. Generally, the earth and heaven's creations have manuscript and architectural designs. The whole essence of the manuscript is to reveal the purpose of creation. There is a book called the book of the living, although this has not been shown to the world else, everyone would have the idea of the total number of people that had walked through this world:

"And all that dwell upon the earth shall worship him, whose names are not
written in the book of life of the Lamb slain from the foundation of the world"
(Revelations 13:8 KJV).

Owing to the above scripture, let us talk about some books below.

The Book of Life of the Lamb Slain from the Foundation of the World

This book of the lamb was written before the foundation of the world. It was written to capture the names of the people that will live in the world before they ever come to the world. Anyone that deviates from the originality of intention will surely have their names erased;

"And all that dwell upon the earth shall worship him, whose names
are not written in the book of life of the Lamb slain from the foundation of the world"
(Revelations 13:8 KJV).
"And I saw the dead, small and great, stand before God; and the books were opened:
and another book was opened, which is the book of life: and the dead were judged out of
those things which were written in the books, according to their works. And whosoever
was not found written in the book of life was cast into the lake of fire" (Revelations
20:12, 15 KJV).

15

The book of life is the book written to contain everyone born into this world. When one comes into this world, one needs to associate with the washing of the blood of Jesus to remain living and recognized in heaven. Sin and its demonic nature and attitudes are persistent when there is no identification with Christ. This is why the Psalmist said:

"Let them be blotted out of the book of the living, and not be written with the righteous"
(Psalm 69:28 KJV).

Failure to identify with the righteousness of Christ means the blood of Jesus will wipe the name off:

"Yet now, if thou wilt forgive their sin--; and if not, blot me, I pray thee, out of thy book which thou hast written. And the Lord said unto Moses, Whosoever hath sinned against me, him will I blot out of my book" (Exodus 32:32-33 KJV).

Moses said if God will not forgive their sins, then He should blot out his name from the book of life and God said I only erase sinners' names. We become a citizen of Zion through our identification with Christ and not just being born into this world. The above scripture depicts that by and by written names will reduce due to sin. Those whose sins have not been forgiven through identification with Christ will have their names erased from the book, and they will not be qualified to live in Zion. The blood of the slain lamb checkmates the book of life and erases sinners from the book. Once it is erased then it will no longer be found:

"And I saw the dead, small and great, stand before God; and the books were opened: and another book was opened, which is the book of life: and the dead were judged out of those things which were written in the books, according to their works. And whosoever was not found written in the book of life was cast into the lake of fire"
(Revelations 20:12, 15 KJV).

There is a clear difference between the book of life and the books. According to the scripture:
"I saw the dead, both great and small, standing before God's throne. And the books were opened, including the Book of Life. And the dead were judged according to what they had done, as recorded in the books" (Revelations 20:12 NLT).

The books including the book of life were stated above. The book of life is the register for those living in the world. On the other hand, the books are for judging the dead according to what they had done, as recorded in the books. Works are only recorded in the books and not in the book of life.

Accepting Christ is compulsory after being born into this world. That is our compulsory second birth, proof of remaining in the book of life, and confirmation of citizenship:

"I will make mention of Rahab and Babylon to them that know me: behold Philistia, and Tyre, with Ethiopia; this man was born there. And of Zion it shall be said, This and that man was born in her: and the highest himself shall establish her" (Psalm 87:4-5 KJV). "When the Lamb broke the seventh seal on the scroll, there was silence throughout heaven for about half an hour" (Revelations 8:1 NLT).

The Books and the Book of Remembrance

Our works on the earth are recorded by angels in the books. The fact that we don't see where our works are written is not enough to think our works are not recorded. They are written in different books in heaven.

"I saw the dead, both great and small, standing before God's throne. And the books were opened, including the Book of Life. And the dead were judged according to what they had done, as recorded in the books" (Revelations 20:12 NLT).

Whatever we do is recorded in the books. Our works will be tested by fire after this world: *"Every man's work shall be made manifest: for the day shall declare it, because it shall be revealed by fire; and the fire shall try every man's work of what sort it is" (1 Corinthians 3:13 KJV).*

There are many books for different purposes. There is a book that only captures the thoughts and talk of the righteous about the Lord, followed by a memorable deed. The book of remembrance is where some work of every man is considered by God and written for great reward. The qualification for this is to have one's name confirmed by the lamb's blood to meet the righteousness criterion required to remain in the book of life. This spiritual vade mecum is only replete with the details of those who fear the Lord and have the continual habit of thinking about Him. Look at what the scripture says:
"Then they that feared the Lord spake often one to another: and the Lord hearkened, and heard it, and a book of remembrance was written before him for them that feared the Lord, and that thought upon his name. And they shall be mine, saith the Lord of hosts, in

that day when I make up my jewels; and I will spare them, as a man spareth his own son that serveth him. Then shall ye return, and discern between the righteous and the wicked, between him that serveth God and him that serveth him not" (Malachi 3:16-18 KJV).

This is the book of memorable and faithful deeds. It is the way God rewards His faithful. It is a repayment quarto. It is a rich spiritual book of chronicles. It's like what the book of Esther spoke about *Mordecai*:

"That night the king could not sleep; so he ordered the book of the chronicles, the record of his reign, to be brought in and read to him. It was found recorded there that Mordecai had exposed Bigthana and Teresh, two of the king's officers who guarded the doorway, who had conspired to assassinate King Xerxes" (Esther 6:1-2 KJV).

The Lord Himself said I will repay every man according to the work of His hand:
"Look, I am coming soon! My reward is with me, and I will give to each person according to what they have done" (Revelations 22:12 KJV).
This can only be possible because the works are recorded. They are kept intact. They cannot be ignored or forgotten in the Spirit realm.

ii. The Heavenly-Tongue Writing
There are diverse writings in the spirit realm. These writings are done by the supernatural ability of God and willed into every of His eternal architectural design. This is the reason heaven's foundations have writings:

"And had a wall great and high, and had twelve gates, and at the gates twelve angels, and names written thereon, which are the names of the twelve tribes of the children of Israel: On the east three gates; on the north three gates; on the south three gates; and on the west three gates. And the wall of the city had twelve foundations, and in them the names of the twelve apostles of the Lamb" (Revelations 21:12-14 KJV).

Heaven's buildings have writings. Spirits living in heaven have writings upon them in the form of a dog tag. These writings are for clear identifications and nomenclature in heaven. A lot of records exist in Heaven. These records are written so that proportionate rewards will be attracted by the subjects. Heaven has different scrolls well written and sealed. You can simply differentiate every building, spirit, and event through their writings.
"And they will see his face, and his name will be written on their foreheads"

18

(Revelations 22:4 KJV).

It is beautiful to know that angels can write the same way God does. God writes through His breath, tongue, and finger. The writing through God's breath is a form of tongue impression. All of God's creation came from His breath or spoken words:

"And God said, Let there be light: and there was light. And God saw the light, that it was good: and God divided the light from the darkness. And God called the light Day, and the darkness he called Night. And the evening and the morning were the first day. And God said, Let there be a firmament in the midst of the waters, and let it divide the waters from the waters" (Genesis 1: 3-6 KJV).

"My heart is inditing a good matter: I speak of the things which I have made touching the king: my tongue is the pen of a ready writer" (Psalm 45:1 KJV).

In the time of Moses, God did not just use only tongue to write and establish all of creation, Heaven, and laws He also used His finger:

"And he gave unto Moses, when he had made an end of communing with him upon mount Sinai, two tables of testimony, tables of stone, written with the finger of God" (Exodus 31:18 KJV).

Remember that God is a consuming fire. If a man will write on tablets of stone, there must be an iota of intense fire and heat in his hands that can bore impeccable lines on the stones. God wrote in Moses' language. The writing was clear to Moses. How did God know how to write in Moses's tongue "the Hebrew tongue"? All languages can be spoken by God without an exemption to the Hebrew tongue! He is the creator of all.

In addition, an angel also wrote with his finger and no man could interpret except Daniel:
"In the same hour came forth fingers of a man's hand, and wrote over against the candlestick upon the plaister of the wall of the king's palace: and the king saw the part of the hand that wrote. Then the king's countenance was changed, and his thoughts troubled him, so that the joints of his loins were loosed, and his knees smote one against another. The king cried aloud to bring in the astrologers, the Chaldeans, and the soothsayers. And the king spake, and said to the wise men of Babylon, Whosoever shall

read this writing, and shew me the interpretation thereof, shall be clothed with scarlet, and have a chain of gold about his neck, and shall be the third ruler in the kingdom. Then came in all the king's wise men: but they could not read the writing, nor make known to the king the interpretation thereof" (Daniel 5: 5-8 KJV).

What kind of language is this that no man can interpret? It was not part of the languages of the earth, yet was written on the wall. No man can be able to interpret or read and understand a writing that you have not learned or a language that you do not speak. However, Daniel in his days interpreted the divine writing through the help of the Spirit of God:

"And thou his son, O Belshazzar, hast not humbled thine heart, though thou knewest all this; But hast lifted up thyself against the Lord of heaven; and they have brought the vessels of his house before thee, and thou, and thy lords, thy wives, and thy concubines, have drunk wine in them; and thou hast praised the gods of silver, and gold, of brass, iron, wood, and stone, which see not, nor hear, nor know: and the God in whose hand thy breath is, and whose are all thy ways, hast thou not glorified:

Then was the part of the hand sent from him; and this writing was written. And this is the writing that was written, Mene, Mene, Tekel, Upharsin. This is the interpretation of the thing: Mene; God hath numbered thy kingdom, and finished it. Tekel; Thou art weighed in the balances, and art found wanting. Peres; Thy kingdom is divided, and given to the Medes and Persians" (Daniel 5:22-28 KJV).

It is surprising to see how an angel sent by God could denote his writing in an unknown language. No man could understand it because it was infrequent in the earthly realm. Such writing can only find interpretation anytime, any day with the spiritually inclined individuals.

Key Activation Prayers

Awesome Holy Spirit, I decree that I develop the inspiration for writing and speaking dynamic tongues. Let this dimension be evident in my life right now. I activate the multi-dimensional power to instruct with writing in the name of the Father, the Son, and the Holy Spirit in Jesus' name. Amen!

Chapter

3

THE MESSENGER ANGELS' DIMENSION OF TONGUES

CHAPTER THREE

THE MESSENGER ANGELS' DIMENSION OF TONGUES

"Father, glorify thy name. Then came there a voice from heaven, saying, I have both glorified it, and will glorify it again. The people therefore, that stood by, and heard it, said that it thundered: others said, An angel spake to him. Jesus answered and said, this voice came not because of me, but for your sakes" (John12:28-31 KJV).

Heaven is the most advanced spiritual civilization and ecosystem. It's the habitation and civilization of angels. In Heaven, the spirit civilization within the ecosystem comes with a God-born hereditary factor, making a spiritual language an inherent thing for perfect communication within the ecosystem. Angels don't need to learn angelic tongues. It was just wired by God into their spiritual DNA. Heaven is a spirit-social and cultural development-organization that is considered the most advanced in all ecosystems including the earth.

When men both young and old including the dumb journey to Heaven, they gain the ability to communicate like angels expressly by the ordinance of God without having to learn the heavenly tongues. They can talk like God and talk with angels. For instance, look at this conversation ensuing below among the twenty-four elders, four beasts, John the beloved, and the one who sat on the throne.

"After this I looked, and, behold, a door was opened in heaven: and the first voice which I heard was as it were of a trumpet talking with me; which said, Come up hither, and I will shew thee things which must be hereafter. And immediately I was in the spirit: and, behold, a throne was set in heaven, and one sat on the throne. And he that sat was to look upon like a jasper and a sardine stone: and there was a rainbow round about the throne, in sight like unto an emerald. And round about the throne were four and twenty seats: and upon the seats, I saw four and twenty elders sitting, clothed in white raiment; and they had on their heads crowns of gold.
And out of the throne proceeded lightnings and thundering and voices: and there were seven lamps of fire burning before the throne, which are the seven Spirits of God. And before the throne there was a sea of glass like unto crystal: and in the midst of the

throne, and round about the throne, were four beasts full of eyes before and behind. And the first beast was like a lion, and the second beast like a calf, and the third beast had a face as a man, and the fourth beast was like a flying eagle. And the four beasts had each of them six wings about him; and they were full of eyes within: and they rest not day and night, saying, Holy, holy, holy, Lord God Almighty, which was, and is, and is to come. And when those beasts give glory and honour and thanks to him that sat on the throne, who liveth for ever and ever, The four and twenty elders fall down before him that sat on the throne, and worship him that liveth for ever and ever, and cast their crowns before the throne, saying, Thou art worthy, O Lord, to receive glory and honour and power: for thou hast created all things, and for thy pleasure they are and were created"
(Revelations 4:2-11 KJV).

Did you observe something here? There was communication with the one on the throne. The four beasts spoke, the twenty-four elders spoke with God, and one of the elders also spoke with John in Heaven. The communication was with perfect understanding. Something worthy of note here is the fact that the four beasts were never schooled on the earth to have understood John, neither the one on the throne nor the twenty-four elders. How then was there perfect communication without anyone in need of an interpreter? This question will be answered in our next outline.

The Tongues of the Messenger Angels in the Spiritual Ecosystem

Angels have unique tongues. This uniqueness is in accordance with Heaven's protocol and civilization. Communication can be verbal, nonverbal, written, visual, or listening. The Spirit's ecosystem is designed by God to follow this order. If there is any difference, it will be just a little so as to accommodate other eternal features. The code of heaven's mode of instruction is structured by God and different from the earth's civilization. Hence, Apostle Paul cleared the air, saying

"Though I speak with the tongues of men and of angels, and have not charity, I am become as sounding brass or a tinkling cymbal" (1 Corinthians 13:1 KJV).

His statement clearly revealed that angels and men have different tongues. However, any believer who has the God factor "the Holy Spirit" can switch tongues like Paul. The one who always makes this possible is the Holy Spirit. Spiritual Men can switch tongues and angels can do the same. Men who do not belong to this realm cannot interpret the tongues and the writings of angels because they are coded. Men's tongues and writings are usually the product of this earthly civilization. It is a set of curricula designed by men as a mode of communication and set of instructions.

The tongues of ministering angels can be heard in two ways:

i.   Men's languages in earthly civilization

Angels can speak men's languages when they are given the legal power and authority to deliver messages on the earth. They can wear men's cloak. Come to the house of humans, eat food, drink water and sleep as well. They can speak the language of any tribe and race to humans. Their voices can be heard in the place of prayers. They can also visit people's houses physically with the appearance of a human being.

ii.   Spiritual tongues of heaven's civilization

Angels can speak coded tongues. These tongues are coded because they are barricaded information. This usually happens if they don't want the people close to a man to hear. It can sound like a rumble of thunder. A sound without meaning; spiritual conundrum sounds. These spiritual tongues of heaven's civilization are obscure, even when natural people hear them, they cannot demystify them. Only spiritual people can relate to it and receive the interpretation.

Below are a few conversations that will beam more light on the tongues of ministering angels and how they can be heard:

The Conversation of Angels with the Old Saints

The scriptures are replete with information on angelic assignments and a number of examples of angels sent to minister to men at different times. These angels communicated with men in different places, and at different times. Most of the people being communicated with are of different races, tribes, and ethnicity, yet the angels could speak their languages. Why is it like this? Let's examine some conversations below:

Angel Gabriel's Conversation with Zechariah

The priest Zechariah was spoken to by an angel, the communication was being done with him in the tongue of men; a known tongue. How is this possible, since the two don't live in the same zone of life?

"There was in the days of Herod, the king of Judaea, a certain priest named Zacharias, of the course of Abia: and his wife was of the daughters of Aaron, and her name was Elisabeth. And they were both righteous before God, walking in all the commandments

and ordinances of the Lord blameless. And they had no child, because that Elisabeth was barren, and they both were now well stricken in years. And it came to pass, that while he executed the priest's office before God in the order of his course, according to the custom of the priest's office, his lot was to burn incense when he went into the temple of the Lord. And the whole multitude of the people were praying without at the time of incense. And there appeared unto him an angel of the Lord standing on the right side of the altar of incense. And when Zacharias saw him, he was troubled, and fear fell upon him. But the angel said unto him, Fear not, Zacharias: for thy prayer is heard; and thy wife Elisabeth shall bear thee a son, and thou shalt call his name John. And thou shalt have joy and gladness; and many shall rejoice at his birth. For he shall be great in the sight of the Lord, and shall drink neither wine nor strong drink; and he shall be filled with the Holy Ghost, even from his mother's womb. And many of the children of Israel shall he turn to the Lord their God. And he shall go before him in the spirit and power of Elias, to turn the hearts of the fathers to the children, and the disobedient to the wisdom of the just; to make ready a people prepared for the Lord. And Zacharias said unto the angel, Whereby shall I know this? for I am an old man, and my wife well stricken in years. And the angel answering said unto him, I am Gabriel that stand in the presence of God; and am sent to speak unto thee, and to shew thee these glad tidings. And, behold, thou shalt be dumb, and not able to speak, until the day that these things shall be performed, because thou believest not my words, which shall be fulfilled in their season" (Luke 1:5-20 KJV).

You could see the angel's words and Zechariah's response above. The hearing, listening, and speaking demonstrated by the angel and Zechariah are proof of understanding. If angels can hear man, then they can speak man's tongues. People from different races, tribes, and tongues do communicate with angels. They also have proofs that angels hear them or appear to them to give messages. If they can hear, then they can speak. This is possible because of the power of God. So many people reading this book have also had visions and encountered angels ministering to them in their native languages.

Angel Gabriel's Conversation with Mary

Mary had a lifetime opportunity by being visited by an angel. The exciting part of this interaction is that the choice of language chosen by the angel to deliver the good news to her is human language. Mary never spoke the tongue of angels. She interacted with the angel in the language of man; her native tongue.

"And in the sixth month the angel Gabriel was sent from God unto a city of Galilee, named Nazareth, to a virgin espoused to a man whose name was Joseph, of the house of David; and the virgin's name was Mary. And the angel came in unto her, and said, Hail, thou that art highly favoured, the Lord is with thee: blessed art thou among women. And when she saw him, she was troubled at his saying, and cast in her mind what manner of salutation this should be. And the angel said unto her, Fear not, Mary: for thou hast found favour with God. And, behold, thou shalt conceive in thy womb, and bring forth a son, and shalt call his name Jesus. He shall be great, and shall be called the Son of the Highest: and the Lord God shall give unto him the throne of his father David: And he shall reign over the house of Jacob forever; and of his kingdom there shall be no end. Then said Mary unto the angel, How shall this be, seeing I know not a man? And the angel answered and said unto her, The Holy Ghost shall come upon thee, and the power of the Highest shall overshadow thee: therefore also that holy thing which shall be born of thee shall be called the Son of God. And, behold, thy cousin Elisabeth, she hath also conceived a son in her old age: and this is the sixth month with her, who was called barren. For with God nothing shall be impossible. And Mary said, Behold the handmaid of the Lord; be it unto me according to thy word. And the angel departed from her"
(Luke 1:26-38 KJV).

The communication seen above was mutual, clear, and well-understood by the two parties. If you would ask Mary by saying "what is the tongue of angel Gabriel"? Mary would have said my native tongue because I heard him speak in my native tongue. This kind of conversation again is an eye-opener about the tongues of angels.

Abraham And Sarah's Conversation with The Angels

Countless numbers of saints in the Old Testament had the privilege of being visited by angels. Abraham and Sarah are a case study in this scenario. Besides them, there are a good number of people who also had well-documented interactions with angels at different generations. In most of the conversations recorded in the Bible, we could see the consistency of communication and understanding. The fluency and accuracy of their communication and expression of intent were like when a man was speaking to a man. It was expressively homogeneous throughout the Bible except on rare occasions. Angels do speak to people, minister to people, and make known their intentions as they are sent by God. In most cases, we could see an angel like Gabriel speaking to many people from different tribes and races in different generations, and he is being able to speak to them in their various tongues. I have had ministers in my country testify of angels who spoke to them. Some of these angels had spoken to other people in other tribes and races. How is it that they are able to speak the diverse native languages of men? This definitely will have something unique to do with the wisdom of God.

Let us explore further the communications of the Lord with Abraham. According to the scriptures and inferences that were drawn from the communication, God spoke in the native language of Abraham. The tongue with which the Lord spoke with was what gave perfect understanding to Abraham and His wife. The accompanying messenger angels that came with the Lord were also logically dispatched through the same mode of communication as the Lord continued to speak with Abraham.

"And the Lord appeared unto him in the plains of Mamre: and he sat in the tent door in the heat of the day; And he lift up his eyes and looked, and, lo, three men stood by him: and when he saw them, he ran to meet them from the tent door, and bowed himself toward the ground, And said, My Lord, if now I have found favour in thy sight, pass not away, I pray thee, from thy servant: Let a little water, I pray you, be fetched, and wash your feet, and rest yourselves under the tree. And the Lord said, Shall I hide from Abraham that thing which I do; Seeing that Abraham shall surely become a great and mighty nation, and all the nations of the earth shall be blessed in him? For I know him, that he will command his children and his household after him, and they shall keep the way of the Lord, to do justice and judgment; that the Lord may bring upon Abraham that which he hath spoken of him. And the Lord said, Because the cry of Sodom and Gomorrah is great, and because their sin is very grievous; I will go down now, and see whether they have done altogether according to the cry of it, which is come unto me; and if not, I will know. And the men turned their faces from thence, and went toward Sodom: but Abraham stood yet before the Lord. And Abraham drew near, and said, Wilt thou also destroy the righteous with the wicked?" (Genesis 18:1-4, 17-23 KJV).

Now, if you think it was some form of an unknown tongue, imagine when Abraham said to the Lord will thou destroy the righteous with the wicked or when the Lord said why did Sarah laugh, and Sarah denied it:

"And the Lord said unto Abraham, Wherefore did Sarah laugh, saying, Shall I of a surety bear a child, which am old? Is anything too hard for the Lord? At the time appointed I will return unto thee, according to the time of life, and Sarah shall have a son. Then Sarah denied, saying, I laughed not; for she was afraid. And he said, Nay; but thou didst laugh" (Genesis 18:13-15 KJV).

This tells you that Abraham and Sarah spoke in their native tongues with the Lord. This is how God has programmed encounters whether with angels or Himself. Ninety-eight percent of effective communication which lasted beyond a generation was done using this medium.

Angels' conversation With Lot

Lot according to the scripture was a righteous man. God having considered Abraham's petition sent Lot angels who would take him out of the city before the destruction of the city. The communication that ensued between them as a result of the message is what we want to observe here. See what the scripture said below:

"And there came two angels to Sodom at even; and Lot sat in the gate of Sodom: and Lot seeing them rose up to meet them; and he bowed himself with his face toward the ground; And he said, Behold now, my lords, turn in, I pray you, into your servant's house, and tarry all night, and wash your feet, and ye shall rise up early, and go on your ways. And they said, Nay; but we will abide in the street all night. And he pressed upon them greatly; and they turned in unto him, and entered into his house; and he made them a feast, and did bake unleavened bread, and they did eat, And the men said unto Lot, Hast thou here any besides? son in law, and thy sons, and thy daughters, and whatsoever thou hast in the city, bring them out of this place: For we will destroy this place, because the cry of them is waxen great before the face of the Lord; and the Lord hath sent us to destroy it. And Lot went out, and spake unto his sons in law, which married his daughters, and said, Up, get you out of this place; for the Lord will destroy this city. But he seemed as one that mocked unto his sons in law. And when the morning arose, then the angels hastened Lot, saying, Arise, take thy wife, and thy two daughters, which are here; lest thou be consumed in the iniquity of the city. And while he lingered, the men laid hold upon his hand, and upon the hand of his wife, and upon the hand of his two daughters; the Lord being merciful unto him: and they brought him forth, and set him without the city. And it came to pass, when they had brought them forth abroad, that he said, Escape for thy life; look not behind thee, neither stay thou in all the plain; escape to the mountain, lest thou be consumed" (Genesis 19: 2-3, 13-17 KJV).

So much to note from the scriptures we just read. We could see in the above communication that the angels spoke to Lot in a native tongue for effective dissemination of the information. Again, this is a big surprise.

The angels ate food with Lot's family. They played with the kids and the wife and when the morning arose, then the angels hastened Lot saying "arise, take thy wife, and thy two daughters, which are here; lest thou be consumed in the iniquity of the city". To date, this still happens to people on earth. The scripture puts it this way:

"Be not forgetful to entertain strangers: for thereby some have entertained angels unawares" (Hebrews 13:2 KJV).

We need to be careful as angels can appear to us and speak to us in our native tongues. The tongue of angels does not mean it will be unknown else the Bible would not have admonished us to be sensitive to discerning when angels take human form to appear in our world. It means angels can come into the world of men and approach us in the tongues of men. The scriptures are glutted with many examples of such.

An Angel or an Ass?

The wisdom of God is incomparable to none. The wisdom displayed in this scenario is such that can make one question every work of God when they are being beheld. Sometimes, when you look at certain animals, it's almost like they are communicating while they are acting their territorial farce. God can communicate through nature. In this case, it is through an animal. See the scripture below:

"And Balaam rose up in the morning, and saddled his ass, and went with the princes of Moab. And God's anger was kindled because he went: and the angel of the Lord stood in the way for an adversary against him. Now he was riding upon his ass, and his two servants were with him. And the ass saw the angel of the Lord standing in the way, and his sword drawn in his hand: and the ass turned aside out of the way, and went into the field: and Balaam smote the ass, to turn her into the way. But the angel of the Lord stood in a path of the vineyards, a wall being on this side, and a wall on that side. And when the ass saw the angel of the Lord, she thrust herself unto the wall, and crushed Balaam's foot against the wall: and he smote her again. And the angel of the Lord went further, and stood in a narrow place, where was no way to turn either to the right hand or to the left. And when the ass saw the angel of the Lord, she fell down under Balaam: and

Balaam's anger was kindled, and he smote the ass with a staff. And the Lord opened the mouth of the ass, and she said unto Balaam, What have I done unto thee, that thou hast smitten me these three times? And Balaam said unto the ass, Because thou hast mocked me: I would there were a sword in mine hand, for now would I kill thee. And the ass said unto Balaam, Am not I thine ass, upon which thou hast ridden ever since I was thine unto this day? was I ever wont to do so unto thee? and he said, Nay. Then the Lord opened the eyes of Balaam, and he saw the angel of the Lord standing in the way, and his sword drawn in his hand: and he bowed down his head, and fell flat on his face. And the angel of the Lord said unto him, Wherefore hast thou smitten thine ass these three times? behold, I went out to withstand thee, because thy way is perverse before me"
(Numbers 22:21-32 KJV).

There are two things to observe here: the fact that the angel gave the donkey utterance and the fact that the angel also spoke the same tongue with Balaam. These tell you how angels can use even animals to communicate with man. I have seen angels speak through nature like this.

Angels' Tongues In The Place Of Prayers and Meditation

Angels do interrupt our prayers and meditations. Many times, when we are praying or when studying the word, we are visited by angels who communicate to us in our native tongues. Sometimes, the voice goes through the airwave to get to us. We receive those words thinking they are just mere thoughts but far from it. They are words from the throne of God brought to us by angels. The fact that we heard them in our understanding can make it look like it is our mere reasoning and thoughts. Far from it, most of those words are from God's holy angels.

Strategies For Hosting the Angels Of God And Operating In This Dimension

It is possible to speak the tongue of angels just like the donkey did when in actual fact, it was the angel that spoke the tongue of men through the donkey. There are a few things you will need to host the angels of God coming into your world to deliver a message. Being cozy with this realm is a function of knowledge and understanding. No one can operate in this realm without a depth of knowledge, else such persons might be a victim of such manifestation. Several of the old saints who walked with God did so with openness of hearts. They lived righteously. They walked with God without doubts in their hearts. Abraham was a good example of this. Zechariah who was a priest in his days was affected because He lacked the amplitude of knowledge required to host the encounter. Angels are messenger spirits sent from God. You will need the following to master their operations:

i.   The knowledge of who you are now in Christ.
ii.   The knowledge of who angels are.
iii. The knowledge of God's authority backing angelic assignment.
iv.   Regular personal prayer communion.
v.   Association of the God kind.
vi.   Personal walk of faith.
vii. Living a consistent righteous life.
viii. Constant fellowship with the word and meditation.
ix.   Constant fellowship with the saints of God.

The Knowledge of Who You are in Christ

The knowledge of who you are in Christ is essential to walking and operating in the dimension of the tongue of the messenger angels. You are no longer you, but Him:

> *"Therefore, if anyone is in Christ, he is a new creation; old things have passed away; behold, all things have become new" (2 Corinthians 5:17 KJV).*

This revelation is needed to sustain your rank. You are a new creature. You now live permanently in Christ. Now that you are in Him, you share His identity, life, and power:

> *"For you died, and your life is hidden with Christ in God. When Christ who is our life appears, then you also will appear with Him in glory" (Colossians 3:3-4 KJV).*

The life you live is His. So just imagine when an angel appears before you, he is appearing before the life of God. Hallelujah!

You are a loving being. You have become like Him through the love nature that He has given you. It is gotten through the consummation of redemption through His blood. Jesus' personality is what perfectly describes you:

> *"Love has been perfected among us in this: that we may have boldness in the day of judgment; because as He is, so are we in this world"*
> *(1 Corinthians 4:17 KJV).*

We are now exactly like the one who redeemed us. Our value is His worth. The price that was paid for us which is the blood is our worth. We now have a new temple:

"Or do you not know that your body is the temple of the Holy Spirit who is in you, whom you have from God, and you are not your own? For you were bought at a price; therefore glorify God in your body and in your spirit, which are God's" (1 Corinthians 6:19-20 KJV). When dealing with angels on the earth, it is important never to worship them. No holy angels in the realm of God will accept your worship of Him:

> *"Now I, John, saw and heard these things. And when I heard and saw, I fell down to worship before the feet of the angel who showed me these things. Then he said to me, "See that you do not do that. For I am your fellow servant, and of your brethren the prophets, and of those who keep the words of this book. Worship God"*
> *(Revelations 22:8-9 KJV).*

This is a law in the spirit realm. No one should worship any other besides God. When Jesus was tempted with worship by Lucifer, see what happened:

> *"And the devil said unto him, All this power will I give thee, and the glory of them: for that is delivered unto me; and to whomsoever I will I give it. If thou therefore wilt worship me, all shall be thine. And Jesus answered and said unto him, Get thee behind me, Satan: for it is written, Thou shalt worship the Lord thy God, and him only shalt thou serve"* (Luke 4:6-8 KJV).

What Jesus said above in response was the scriptural instruction quoted from the book of Deuteronomy 6:13. It is taboo for anyone carrying Jesus to worship angels.

The Knowledge of Who Angels Are

We need to know how to interact with angels. The Lord has a great plan for us. He wants to guide us into His plans and purposes. To do this, the Lord uses the ministry of angels. Angels are ministering spirits sent from the throne of God: *"And of the angels he saith, Who maketh his angels spirits, and his ministers a flame of fire" (Hebrew 1:7 KJV).* When the devil was done tempting Jesus, the scriptures said angels came and ministered to Him (Mathew 4: 11 KJV). Angels minister to the saints of God. They carry good news from the realms of God to the earthly realm. They are sent to carry out God's agenda here on earth. Sometimes, they get involved in fighting:

> *"And it came to pass that night, that the angel of the Lord went out, and smote in the camp of the Assyrians an hundred fourscore and five thousand: and when they arose*

early in the morning, behold, they were all dead corpses"
(2 Kings 19:35 KJV).

No angel of God will ask you to do anything contrary to the will of God. If any angel would even dare to preach a different gospel to you the bible says he must be accursed. It is declared according to the mind of God. No angel will preach against the kingdom's adoptions. Look at how it is written:

"But though we, or an angel from heaven, preach any other gospel unto you than that which we have preached unto you, let him be accursed" (Galatians 1:8 KJV).

The knowledge and revelation of who angels are is important in that they guide us into knowing what angels do. Angels were contrived by God to carry out specific assignments for God. There are warring angels, good news angels, worship angels, glory angels, throne angels, dominion angels, Cherubs, Seraphs, and so on.

The Knowledge of God's Authority Backing Angelic Assignment

We need to learn to always believe God and His infinite abilities to accomplish anything especially when we receive His words, and upon having confirmed the genuineness of the dissemination source, "the holy messenger angels", it is necessary that we trust God's ability to absolutely do whatever He says. Zechariah was a victim of doubt:

"And Zacharias said unto the angel, Whereby shall I know this? for I am an old man, and my wife well stricken in years. And the angel answering said unto him, I am Gabriel, that stand in the presence of God; and am sent to speak unto thee, and to shew thee these glad tidings. And, behold, thou shalt be dumb, and not able to speak, until the day that these things shall be performed, because thou believest not my words, which shall be fulfilled in their season" (Luke 1:18-20 KJV).

It is generally dangerous not to believe God and murmur against His covenant at any time. This is why the Bible says

"And the LORD heard the voice of your words, and was wroth, and sware, saying, Surely there shall not one of these men of this evil generation see that good land, which I sware to give unto your fathers Deuteronomy" (1:34-35 KJV).

Regular Personal Prayer Communion

It is possible for one to encounter an angel in the place of prayer just like Zechariah when fulfilling the obligation of prayers. If you want to hear the tongues of the messenger angels consistently, cultivate a regular habit of praying earnestly. Look at Jesus' example whenever He withdrew Himself to pray earnestly, He encountered both the voices of the devil and the holy angels of God:

"And Jesus being full of the Holy Ghost returned from Jordan, and was led by the Spirit into the wilderness, Being forty days tempted of the devil. And in those days he did eat nothing: and when they were ended, he afterward hungered *And the devil said unto him, If thou be the Son of God, command this stone that it be made bread*" (Luke 4:1-2 KJV).

Did you see that it was in the place of prayer that He battled with the voice of the demonic angel "the devil"? Afterward, the scripture said "*Then the devil leaveth him, and, behold, angels came and ministered unto him*" *(Matthew 4:11 KJV).*

Again, see another example of when He separated Himself for prayers:

"And he was withdrawn from them about a stone's cast, and kneeled down, and prayed, Saying, Father, if thou be willing, remove this cup from me: nevertheless, not my will, but thine, be done. And there appeared an angel unto him from heaven, strengthening him"
(Luke 23:41-43 KJV).

We can deduct from the two experiences of Jesus that the place of prayer is the place of battling with voices and tongues.

Association of the God Kind

The company being kept by one can also engender certain supernatural manifestation of the abilities of God. Angels can interrupt such gatherings and their practices if they are holy.

"And when they had prayed, the place was shaken where they were assembled together; and they were all filled with the Holy Ghost, and they spake the word of God with boldness" (Acts 4:31 KJV).

Personal Walk of Faith

Our walk of faith can attract the guidance of angels to us. The walk of faith is a divine walk with angelic accompaniment.

"For we walk by faith, not by sight" (2 Corinthians 5:7).

Living A Consistent Righteous Life

Abraham and Lot's lives were such that attracted the visitation of angels. God considered them to be righteous men. For instance, look at Lot at the face of judgement and peril, God had to intervene by sending His angels to him.

"For that righteous man dwelling among them, in seeing and hearing, vexed his righteous soul from day to day with their unlawful deeds" (2 Peter 2:8).

The condition for the intervention of angels in Lot's affair in the land of Sodom was because of his righteousness and association with Abraham's righteousness in walking with God. Righteous living in Christ is a leverage for operating in the messenger angel's dimension of tongues.

"And there came two angels to Sodom at even; and Lot sat in the gate of Sodom: and Lot seeing them rose up to meet them; and he bowed himself with his face toward the ground; And he said, Behold now, my lords, turn in, I pray you, into your servant's house, and tarry all night, and wash your feet, and ye shall rise up early, and go on your ways. And they said, Nay; but we will abide in the street all night. And he pressed upon them greatly; and they turned in unto him, and entered into his house; and he made them a feast, and did bake unleavened bread, and they did eat" (Genesis 19:1-3 KJV).

Constant Fellowship with the Word and Meditation

This is the gateway into mystery revelations in the kingdom of God. No fellowship, no revelation. If you want to enjoy regular visitation of angels, deepen your relationship with Christ, His word and the Holy Spirit.

"That which we have seen and heard declare we unto you, that ye also may have fellowship with us: and truly our fellowship is with the Father, and with his Son Jesus Christ" (1 John 1:3 KJV).

Constant Fellowship with the Saints of God

Cultivating the regular habit of fellowshipping with the matured saints of God has the potential to increase one's experience of the angelic manifestation.

Not forsaking the assembling of ourselves together, as the manner of some is; but exhorting one another: and so much the more, as ye see the day approaching"
(Hebrews 10:25 KJV).

"Now there were in the church that was at Antioch certain prophets and teachers; as Barnabas, and Simeon that was called Niger, and Lucius of Cyrene, and Manaen, which had been brought up with Herod the tetrarch, and Saul. As they ministered to the Lord, and fasted, the Holy Ghost said, Separate me Barnabas and Saul for the work whereunto I have called them"
(Acts 13:1-2 KJV).

The Holy Spirit is seen throughout the scriptures as the angel of the Lord's presence. He invaded the gathering with His voice of direction and guidance as the people engaged in unique fellowship with one another. This is how a believer can enjoy and participate in the messenger angel's dimension of tongues.

Key Activation Prayers
Awesome Holy Spirit, release this fresh grace upon me. Let the angelic tongue dimension of the spirit be activated in my life. Let the operation of this reality begin to find expression in my fellowship in Jesus' name. Amen!

Chapter

THE DIMENSION
OF THE TONGUES
OF MEN

CHAPTER FOUR

THE DIMENSION OF THE TONGUES OF MEN

*"Though I speak with the tongues of men and of angels, and have not charity, I am
become as sounding brass, or a tinkling cymbal."*
(1 Corinthians 13:1 KJV).

The earth's civilization consists of all human social and cultural development and
organization that is considered the most advanced among other horizons created by God.
The way to communicate and understand in this ecosystem is by learning the language of
interaction. The earthly language is what opens and defines the tongue of a natural man. It
happens through learning. If it takes years to learn, how then can angels speak it? Talking of
buying and selling on the earth, or exchanging pleasantries, all of these have to do with
mastering the earthly language as the means of communicating and making our intentions
known. Understanding via listening, speaking, reading and writing is a necessity for
effective interaction in this space.

The tongues of men are learned within the earth for the ease of communication here on earth
with other fellow men. Everyone goes to school to learn it. It can be learned through multiple
sets of curriculum and codes of instruction. We can speak to God and He will hear us through
it. This is the kind of communication that makes our understanding fruitful.

The natural tongues of men are "tongues of fire"

The tongues of men are the native languages with which men communicate with one
another or pray to God. This is also known as the tongue of understanding. Irrespective of
whether a man is born again or not, all men that live on the earth communicate with one
another with this tongue. It is the tongue that the scriptures refer to as the tongue of fire.

*"For in many things we offend all. If any man offend not in word, the same is a perfect man,
and able also to bridle the whole body. Behold, we put bits in the horses' mouths, that they
may obey us; and we turn about their whole body. Behold also the ships, which though they
be so great, and are driven of fierce winds, yet are they turned about with a very small helm,
whithersoever the governor listeth. Even so the tongue is a little member, and boasteth*

great things. Behold, how great a matter a little fire kindleth! And the tongue is a fire, a world of iniquity: so is the tongue among our members, that it defileth the whole body, and setteth on fire the course of nature; and it is set on fire of hell. For every kind of beasts, and of birds, and of serpents, and of things in the sea, is tamed, and hath been tamed of mankind: But the tongue can no man tame; it is an unruly evil, full of deadly poison. Therewith bless we God, even the Father; and therewith curse we men, which are made after the similitude of God. Out of the same mouth proceedeth blessing and cursing. My brethren, these things ought not so to be" (James 3:2-10 KJV).

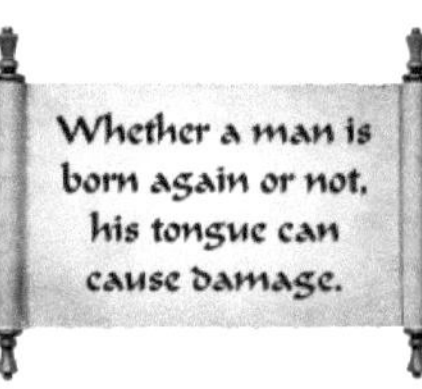

The tongue of man is full of fire. The fact that it can speak evil and good from the same source is a major challenge. You cannot underestimate the power of the tongue in setting ablaze or in building things. Whether a man is born again or not, his tongue can cause damage.

As earlier stated, the tongue of men is the legally approved mode of communication on this planet earth. A very clear disparity can be understudied as people emigrate from one location to different locations on the earth. If one is found in locations with different languages, communication becomes difficult due to a lack of understanding of the language of the new place. Now, imagine if an angel from heaven is to bring messages from heaven to the earth without understanding the language of the earth or the location. How will he communicate or deliver the message? The world of man is chock-full of man's methods of communication such as telex, email, text, telephone, and other means. It will be very hard for an ignorant intruder to break into another man's system of information without understanding the pattern, security and methods of communication. Communication modes preserve information access and storage.

When someone from Tunisia stands to pray together with another from China, the first thing to note is that their individual request and desire will be hidden from each other and undisclosed due to language barrier. It can only be revealed if interpreted. If anyone of them must be built up and edified it has to be in the tongue of understanding; the native tongue or the tongue of men. This is the reason the scripture says *"What is the conclusion then? I will pray with the spirit, and I will also pray with understanding. I will sing with the spirit, and I will also sing with the understanding"* (1 Corinthians 14: 15 KJV).

The tongue of men is a tongue fashioned for understanding among men. But, it is also understood by God. Even though it can take many years for men to learn a language, it does not take God anything at all. He understands all tongues and languages.

All men who walked through the earth in the Old Testament majorly spoke to God in their regular earthly language; the one they learned from their various schools. They never bothered whether God would need someone to teach Him. They spoke in their understanding and God heard them. You might ask, who taught God all the languages of the earth since the languages or the diverse tongues were not in existence when He created heaven and earth? God is the omniscient who created all things. He has power over all that He created. Everything created came out of His inspiration. They are known and well discerned within the realm of His inspiration.

"In my distress I cried to the Lord, And He heard me" (Psalm 120: 1 KJV).

The Energy in the Natural Tongue

There are positive and negative energies in the tongue of a natural man. When he speaks, he can either release positive or negative energies. What he releases is dependent on what word he is speaking. What then is the energy in the natural tongue? It is the power! This power of the natural tongue can destroy or make alive at any time. This is a reflection of the positive and the negative energies. This power is the energy that can convert and be converted into so many things when it is being used in the right way.

Proverbs 18:21 says *"Death and life are in the power of the tongue: and they that love it shall eat the fruit thereof"*.
Death is a negative energy while life is a positive energy. Most troubles are a result of the negative energies that come out of the tongues: *"Whoso keepeth his mouth and his tongue keepeth his soul from troubles" (Proverbs 21:23 KJV)*. Keep your life out of trouble by releasing positive energy from your tongue. Confess the scriptures every time and see the Lord change your stories.

Using Your Tongue the God Way

It is very important to use your tongue in the right way, and in the God way every time. This is the only way to see good days, if you ever desire to see one:
"For he that will love life, and see good days, let him refrain his tongue from evil, and his lips that they speak no guile" (1 Peter 3:10 KJV). Not using your tongue right every time can

lead you into destroying yourself, things, and the people around you. This is why the scripture says:

"Let no corrupt communication proceed out of your mouth, but that which is good to the use of edifying, that it may minister grace unto the hearers" (Ephesians 4:29 KJV). If it does not edify then it can destroy because to edify means to build.

On the other hand, using your tongue in the right way can make your destiny and open the portals of greatness for you. Just as Proverbs 18:21 says *"Death and life are in the power of the tongue: and they that love it shall eat the fruit thereof"*. Consider the following points, they are the ways of using your tongues in the right way;

i. Make the right confession always.

    "Let no corrupt communication proceed out of your mouth, but that which is good to the use of edifying, that it may minister grace unto the hearers" (Ephesians 4:29 KJV).

ii. Don't joke with negative words because there is no joke in the spirit realm.

    "Let there be no filthiness and silly talk, or coarse [obscene or vulgar] joking, because such things are not appropriate [for believers]; but instead speak of your thankfulness [to God]" (Ephesians 5: 4 AMP).

iii. Be slow to speak.

    "Wherefore, my beloved brethren, let every man be swift to hear, slow to speak, slow to wrath" (James 1:19 KJV).

iv. Labor to use your words aright.

    "The tongue of the wise useth knowledge aright: but the mouth of fools poureth out foolishness" (Proverbs 15:2 KJV).

v. Guard yourself with knowledge.

    "The tongue of the wise useth knowledge aright" (Proverbs 15:2a KJV).

vi. Don't backbite with your tongue, it is like the evil rain.

    "The north wind driveth away rain: so doth an angry countenance a backbiting tongue" (Proverbs 25:23 KJV).

vii. Don't use your tongue for tale-bearing.

    "Where no wood is, there the fire goeth out: so where there is no talebearer, the strife "ceaseth (Proverbs 26:20 KJV).

viii. Avoid piercing your soul with your words.

"There is that speaketh like the piercings of a sword: but the tongue of the wise is health" (Proverbs 12:18 KJV).

ix. Be mindful of your words because you will give an account of every word.

"But I tell you, on the day of judgment people will have to give an accounting for every careless or useless word they speak. For by your words [reflecting your spiritual condition] you will be justified and acquitted of the guilt of sin; and by your words [rejecting Me] you will be condemned and sentenced." (Mathew 12:36-37 AMP).

Racial and Tribal Tongues of Men on the Lips of Angels

It is important to know that for the sake of the love of God in guiding men, God can send His angels to all tribes and all races. They are sent to people so that they can correct the ways of men in accordance with the will of God. The dimension of the tongue of men is majorly for man, but the angels of God also do communicate in the tongues of men to bring messages to the men on earth. These angels being sent can speak the tongue of every tribe in every race.

"Be not forgetful to entertain strangers: for thereby some have entertained angels unawares" (Hebrews 13:2 KJV).

Certain angels have walked through the earth. They entered into people's homes without the people knowing because they spoke in earthly languages and were probably dressed like humans. Look at the account of Gideon in the scriptures below:

"Now the Angel of the Lord came and sat under the terebinth tree which was in Ophrah, which belonged to Joash the Abiezrite, while his son Gideon threshed wheat in the winepress, in order to hide it from the Midianites. And the Angel of the Lord appeared to him, and said to him, "The Lord is with you, you mighty man of valor!" Gideon said to Him, "O my lord, if the Lord is with us, why then has all this happened to us? And where are all His miracles which our fathers told us about, saying, 'Did not the Lord bring us up from Egypt?' But now the Lord has forsaken us and delivered us into the hands of the Midianites." Then the Lord turned to him and said, "Go in this might of yours, and you shall save Israel from the hand of the Midianites. Have I not sent you?"
(Judges 6:11-14 KJV).

The angel came and sat down, dressed like a normal human, and began to speak in Gideon's native language. Gideon also spoke back to the angel. The communication was smooth. No need for an interpreter of the angel's tongue. Zechariah had another encounter that showed clearly how angels can appear to people in this age and time and what tongue they can speak:

"And there appeared unto him an angel of the Lord standing on the right side of the altar of incense. And when Zacharias saw him, he was troubled, and fear fell upon him. But the angel said unto him, Fear not, Zacharias: for thy prayer is heard; and thy wife Elisabeth shall bear thee a son, and thou shalt call his name John. And thou shalt have joy and gladness; and many shall rejoice at his birth. For he shall be great in the sight of the Lord, and shall drink neither wine nor strong drink; and he shall be filled with the Holy Ghost, even from his mother's womb. And many of the children of Israel shall he turn to the Lord their God. And he shall go before him in the spirit and power of Elias, to turn the hearts of the fathers to the children, and the disobedient to the wisdom of the just; to make ready a people prepared for the Lord. And Zacharias said unto the angel, Whereby shall I know this? for I am an old man, and my wife well stricken in years. And the angel answering said unto him, I am Gabriel, that stand in the presence of God; and am sent to speak unto thee, and to shew thee these glad tidings. And, behold, thou shalt be dumb, and not able to speak, until the day that these things shall be performed, because thou believest not my words, which shall be fulfilled in their season"
(Luke 1:5-20 KJV).

Over the years, we have seen throughout the Christian communities that various testimonies of believers depict that angels do appear to Christians. Most of the testimonies we receive from believers across the world show certain evidence that God sends His angels to people and the angels sent do speak the languages of the people for easy acceptance of the messages they are supposed to deliver. God almighty Himself also operates like this. Whenever He comes to the world, He speaks the native language of men. A good example is when the Lord appeared to Joshua as the *Commander of the army of the Lord:*

"And it came to pass, when Joshua was by Jericho, that he lifted his eyes and looked, and behold, a Man stood opposite him with His sword drawn in His hand. And Joshua went to Him and said to Him, "Are You for us or for our adversaries?" So He said, "No, but as Commander of the army of the Lord I have now come." And Joshua fell on his face to the earth and worshiped, and said to Him, "What does my Lord say to His servant?" Then the Commander of the Lord's army said to Joshua,

"Take your sandal off your foot, for the place where you stand is holy."
And Joshua did so" (Joshua 5: 13-15 KJV).

Do not be afraid nor anxious to see angels or to hear angels talk to you. God is the one who sends angels to us, only be sensitive.

Praying With The Tongues Of Men "Understanding"

Whenever you are to pray to God in the tongues of men, do it with scriptures on your lips. The scriptures are the secrets to communicating the divine power from the tongues of men. The word of God is the constitution guiding the spirit realm and everything that God has created.

"What is it then? I will pray with the spirit, and I will pray with the understanding also:
I will sing with the spirit, and I will sing with the understanding also"
(1 Corinthians 14:14 KJV).

The word "understanding" as used here is the tongue of men or their native languages. Be conscious that when you are praying with this tongue, angels can communicate with the same to you through the airwaves. You should be mature enough to differentiate the tongue from yours and the inference of your thoughts.

Key Activation Prayers

Awesome Holy Spirit, come upon me with your fresh power, activate this reality right now. Grant me grace to elevate into this reality in Jesus' name. Amen!

Chapter

5

THE DIMENSION OF THE UNKNOWN TONGUE

CHAPTER FIVE

THE DIMENSION OF THE UNKNOWN TONGUE

"These miracles will happen when people believe in me. On my behalf, they will send bad spirits out of people. They will speak new languages."
(Mark 16:17 Easy English).

In the mind of God, the purpose of the unknown tongue is communication. Tongues are a coded spiritual language. When we speak with the unknown tongues, we are speaking to God or spirits. If not, our utterances will have no meaning or quality of expression in the earthly civilization, because it does not conform to their standard of language. Everyone who speaks in tongues or desires to speak in spiritual tongues should know that the essence is communication with God. Therefore, the spiritual tongue is a form of language, the language for connecting with spirits in the earthly horizon or spiritual horizon.

If spiritual tongues have no meaning, then they would have been gibberish. It does not resemble gibberish because the visible beings in the spirit realm can understand what we are saying, especially God and the angel of his presence. Significantly, the bible says

"For he that speaketh in an unknown tongue speaketh not unto men, but unto God: for no man understandeth him; howbeit in the spirit he speaketh mysteries. He that speaketh in an unknown tongue edifieth himself; but he that prophesieth edifieth the church"
(1 Corinthians 14:2, 4 KJV).

The content of our communication in the tongue is called "mystery" to a natural man because it is communication done in the spirit. God is the monarch of the spirit's ecosystem. Only spirit can relate to the code of communication of that community. One who does not belong to that ecosystem may never get to know what has been said. It will remain a mystery. When we speak, we utter swift instructions to the angel of his presence in the spiritual civilization. This makes things happen fast. The angel of God's presence obeys quickly. God himself gets to hear the pure outpouring of our hearts to Him. With speaking in tongues, the soul's hidden agenda is made known to God with or without our consent and knowledge.

Speaking in tongues is releasing a set of codes. God himself does the same. When He spoke to Saul, the people with him saw the light but they did not hear the voice. Paul said

"And they that were with me saw indeed the light, and were afraid; but they heard not the voice of him that spake to me. And I said, What shall I do, Lord? And the Lord said unto me, Arise, and go into Damascus; and there it shall be told thee of all things which are appointed for thee to do" (Acts 22:9-10). How can God be speaking and others not hear? Another example is Jesus when He was with the people He said:

"Father, glorify thy name. Then came there a voice from heaven, saying, I have both glorified it, and will glorify it again. The people therefore, that stood by, and heard it, said that it thundered: others said, an angel spake to him. Jesus answered and said, This voice came not because of me, but for your sakes. Now is the judgment of this world: now shall the prince of this world be cast out. And I, if I be lifted up from the earth, will draw all men unto me" (John12:28-32 KJV).

Did you notice the bible said a voice came to Him? How come they said "it thundered when it was actually a voice that spoke?" That is exactly what tongues look like; it looks like the meaningless sound of a rushing mighty wind! God according to the scripture above coded the information. The details were hidden. It was Jesus who gave them an insight of what was said, saying *"this voice came not because of me, but for your sakes. Now is the judgment of this world: now shall the prince of this world be cast out. And I, if I be lifted up from the earth, will draw all men unto me".* He interpreted what was said. Meanwhile, what was said remained Gibberish. Does God speak in tongues? Yes!

Prophecy and Interpretation "The Diversity of the Unknown Tongues"

What is called prophecy is the tongue. Prophecy is an utterance of a divine message rendered in the tongue of earthly civilization. Those who live in the ecosystem can relate to it. If a prophecy is not tongues it will not be understood by a natural man. A prophecy is a form of tongue, it is a tongue carrying a divine message in the voice code of a natural man for easy acceptance of the angelic instructions. The transmutation of tongues into prophecy can be seen below;

"He that speaketh in an unknown tongue edifieth himself; but he that prophesieth edifieth the church. I would that ye all spake with tongues but rather that ye prophesied: for greater is he that prophesieth than he that speaketh with tongues, except he interpret, that the church may receive edifying" (1 Corinthians 14:5 KJV).

Tongues' transmutation into prophecy is through interpretation. What we call prophecy is a divine interpretation on the tongue of a natural man. When interpretation is added to speaking in tongues it becomes "a prophecy". According to the above scripture, prophecy is edification; a building up and strengthening of someone through words. Edification comes through the understanding of the spoken language. The word edification means to instruct to improve the person. It means being raised and energized intellectually. This can only happen when you are learned in the language of this earthly civilization, knowing what is being said. The aftermath of this kind of understanding is an intellectual improvement. Hence, tongues are un-interpreted prophecies. Meanwhile, prophecy is interpreted in tongues. We can also say tongues are a form of divine message yet to be interpreted, while prophecy is a divine message revealed through interpretation.

The message of Jesus in the book of *Mark 16:17* Easy English says… *"These miracles will happen when people believe in me. On my behalf, they will send bad spirits out of people. They will speak new languages"*. Meaning, even when it is time to send out spirits, they can speak in new languages to instruct the demons, or the people to perform miracles.

The prophecy of Prophet Joel in the book of Acts 2:17 KJV says *"And it shall come to pass in the last days, saith God, I will pour out of my Spirit upon all flesh: and your sons and your daughters shall prophesy, and your young men shall see visions, and your old men shall dream dreams"*.

This prophecy did not capture speaking in tongues. Yet they spoke in tongues. This means what prophet Joel said was implicit. It had an undertone. The tongue was also implied in the prophecy. Peter affirmed, "this is what was said by the prophet Joel". I wonder when Joel said they will speak with new tongues. Let us see the manifestation of the prophecy;

And there appeared unto them cloven tongues like as of fire, and it sat upon each of them. And they were all filled with the Holy Ghost, and began to speak with other tongues, as the Spirit gave them utterance.

And there were dwelling at Jerusalem Jews, devout men, out of every nation under heaven. Now when this was noised abroad, the multitude came together, and were confounded, because that every man heard them speak in his own language. And they were all amazed and marvelled, "saying one to another, Behold, are not all these which speak Galilaeans? And how hear we every man in our own tongue, wherein we were born? Parthians, and Medes, and Elamites, and the dwellers in Mesopotamia, and in Judaea, and Cappadocia, in Pontus, and Asia, Phrygia, and Pamphylia, in Egypt, and in the parts of Libya about Cyrene, and strangers of Rome, Jews and proselytes, Cretes and Arabians, we do hear them speak in our tongues the wonderful works of God. And they were all amazed, and were in doubt, saying one to another, what meaneth this? Others mocking said, these men are full of new wine. But Peter, standing up with the eleven, lifted up his voice, and said unto them, Ye men of Judaea, and all ye that dwell at Jerusalem, be this known unto you, and hearken to my words: For these are not drunken, as ye suppose, seeing it is but the third hour of the day. But this is that which was spoken by the prophet Joel; And it shall come to pass in the last days, saith God, I will pour out of my Spirit upon all flesh: and your sons and your daughters shall prophesy, and your young men shall see visions, and your old men shall dream dreams"
(Acts 2: 3-17 KJV).

The scripture above said, "*And there appeared unto them cloven tongues like as of fire, and it sat upon each of them. And they were all filled with the Holy Ghost, and began to speak with other tongues, as the Spirit gave them utterance*". The utterance according to the scripture included interpretation transmitted to the hearers. This is exactly what propelled many of the hearers to say to another, "*Behold, are not all these which speak Galileans? And how hear we every man in our own tongue, wherein we were born? Parthians, and Medes, and Elamites, and the dwellers in Mesopotamia, and in Judaea, and Cappadocia, in Pontus, and Asia, Phrygia, and Pamphylia, in Egypt, and in the parts of Libya about Cyrene, and strangers of Rome, Jews and proselytes, Cretes and Arabians, we do hear them speak in our tongues the wonderful works of God*". The hearers were all given interpretations by the spirit. Hence, the disciples' tongues metamorphose into prophecy in the ears of the hearers. Think about it!

Why Is It Called An Unknown Tongue?
It is called unknown because it is peculiar to our salvation. Angels speak in diverse tongues; tongues of men and angelic unknown tongues. However, we need to know that for the believers, an unknown tongue is a tongue uttered in the Spirit. It is speaking mysteries to

God in the spirit. The Bible says "no man understands him but the Spirit does". If it is done in the spirit then it can be heard and understood by spirits because it is uttered in the spirit. The scripture says *"For he that speaketh in an unknown tongue speaketh not unto men, but unto God: for no man understandeth him; howbeit in the spirit he speaketh mysteries" (1 Corinthians 14:2 KJV)*. It is called an unknown tongue because natural men do not know it. However, it can be known only through the interpretation of the tongue. Interpretation of tongues comes through the Holy Spirit and Angelic help. Angels do bring the meaning of words to us. Check the scripture below:

"And when the ass saw the angel of the Lord, she thrust herself unto the wall, and crushed Balaam's foot against the wall: and he smote her again. And the angel of the Lord went further, and stood in a narrow place, where was no way to turn either to the right hand or to the left. And when the ass saw the angel of the Lord, she fell down under Balaam: and Balaam's anger was kindled, and he smote the ass with a staff. And the Lord opened the mouth of the ass, and she said unto Balaam, What have I done unto thee, that thou hast smitten me these three times? And Balaam said unto the ass, Because thou hast mocked me: I would there were a sword in mine hand, for now would I kill thee. And the ass said unto Balaam, Am not I thine ass, upon which thou hast ridden ever since I was thine unto this day? was I ever wont to do so unto thee? and he said, Nay. Then the Lord opened the eyes of Balaam, and he saw the angel of the Lord standing in the way, and his sword drawn in his hand: and he bowed down his head, and fell flat on his face. And the angel of the Lord said unto him, Wherefore hast thou smitten thine ass these three times? behold, I went out to withstand thee, because thy way is perverse before me" (Numbers 22:21-32 KJV).

The Lord through the angel of His presence gave the voice of man to the Ass. This is how angels can carry out the agenda of God concerning the interpretation of tongues. Angels can stand close to man to bring words of interpretation to man concerning unknown tongues.

Receiving the Gift of Speaking In Tongues

Speaking in tongues is an effective way to communicate directly with God. The scripture says *"For he that speaketh in an unknown tongue speaketh not unto men, but unto God: for no man understandeth him; howbeit in the spirit he speaketh mysteries"* (1 Corinthians 14:2 KJV). Speaking in tongues is known as praying in the Holy Ghost and it's also regarded as our most holy faith *"But ye, beloved, building up yourselves on your most holy faith, praying in the Holy Ghost" (Jude 1:20 KJV)*. There are four ways to receive the gift:

i.   You can pray by yourself to receive this gift.

ii.   Spoken words without laying on of hands can release the gift.

iiii.   Hands can be laid on you to receive the gift.

iv.   The gift can come upon you unconsciously while you are studying and praying.

These are what I call direct and indirect ways to receive the gifts of speaking in tongues. Believers can take advantage of this measure to receive the Holy Ghost and His gift of speaking in tongues. Let us take a look at a sterling example of Paul's experience below:

"And it came to pass, that, while Apollos was at Corinth, Paul having passed through the upper coasts came to Ephesus: and finding certain disciples, He said unto them, Have ye received the Holy Ghost since ye believed? And they said unto him, We have not so much as heard whether there be any Holy Ghost. And he said unto them, Unto what then were ye baptized? And they said, Unto John's baptism. Then said Paul, John verily baptized with the baptism of repentance, saying unto the people, that they should believe on him which should come after him, that is, on Christ Jesus. When they heard this, they were baptized in the name of the Lord Jesus. And when Paul had laid his hands upon them, the Holy Ghost came on them; and they spake with tongues, and prophesied" (Acts 19:1-6 KJV).

The experience of Paul in the scripture above typically described one of the salient points mentioned above. Acting on any of those points as the Holy ghost may desire and require of anyone is proof of the readiness to travel on the journey of the baptism.

When We Speak in Tongues, We Build Ourselves

There is a building up that takes place in the place of prayers. According to the scripture, we are built as a mighty tower and edifice when we pray in an unknown tongue:

"But ye, beloved, building up yourselves on your most holy faith, praying in the Holy Ghost" (Jude 1:20 KJV).

According to the scripture above, the word building in Greek is "epoikodomeo" meaning to build upon. What are we building? We build upon our faith level when we pray in tongues. It is a way to increase our faith action. It helps us to verbalize our faith in the spirit for effective change. 1 Corinthians 14: 4 says *"He that speaketh in an unknown tongue edifieth himself;*

but he that prophesieth edifieth the church ". The word "edifies" in the above means to build up. In Greek, it is "oikodomeo" metaphorically meaning to promote growth in Christian wisdom and piety. It also means to build a house, erect a building, rebuild and repair or restore and establish. These tell us that we can become established in spiritual wisdom when we speak in tongues. We build our foundation solid through this reality, and nothing can pull us down. This is how we grow besides hearing the word. Our spiritual muscles are developed. We become the epitome of spiritual giants.

Key Activation Prayers

Awesome Holy Spirit, come upon me with your fresh power now. Release your anointing upon me with the evidence of speaking in tongues. Let the burning fire fall upon me. Let the gift of speaking in tongues be activated in Jesus' name. Amen!

Chapter

THE DIMENSION OF THE HEART TONGUE

CHAPTER SIX

THE DIMENSION OF THE HEART TONGUE

"Curse not the king, no not in thy thought; and curse not the rich in thy bedchamber: for a bird of the air shall carry the voice, and that which hath wings shall tell the matter"
(Ecclesiastes 10:20 KJV).

Whatever has the ability to release a word or voice is a tongue. The heart is like a pen that writes every second. It is ever ready to talk in tongues. There are two tongues in the body of a

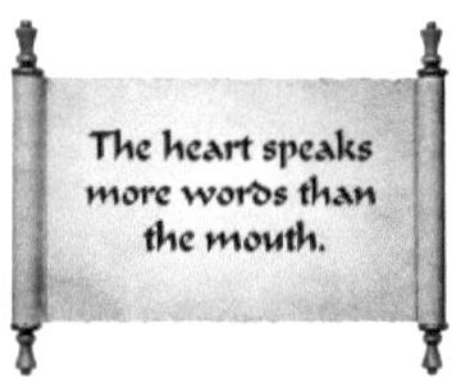

human. The heart tongue and the mouth tongue. The two of them are organs of speech. Thoughts are voices. They are usually produced from the heart before they proceed to the mouth. The hearts are tongues echoing silent inaudible words. The words written and uttered by the heart are more than what the tongue utters at times. The heart is an inner tongue echoing things or words to the owner on the inside. Those words are very loud and can be louder than when they are spoken by someone close to you. The heart speaks more words than the mouth. The mouth can still tame some things, but the heart tongue is harder to be tamed. The heart produces a word to be heard audibly by its owner "the speaker" only, while the tongue produces words to be heard audibly by the speaker and the listener. This is why our opening text says *"Curse not the king, no not in thy thought; and curse not the rich in thy bedchamber: for a bird of the air shall carry the voice, and that which hath wings shall tell the matter" (Ecclesiastes 10:20 KJV). So,* thoughts are voices produced by the inner tongue. They can be carried by winged beings, angels or demons.

The psalmist also says *"My heart is indicting a good matter: I speak of the things which I have made touching the king: my tongue is the pen of a ready writer" (Psalm 45:1 KJV).* According to him, it was his inner voice "the heart" that was indicting a good matter which made his tongue the pen of a ready writer. The heart is a writing pen as much as the tongue is a writing pen. The heart tongue can only be heard by self while the mouth tongue can be heard by everyone around. What the inner tongue perceives can be communicated in different ways; through speaking, writing, or gesticulations. The scripture says *"God is able to do exceeding abundantly above all we can ever ask or <u>think according to the power that</u>*

works in us " (Ephesians 3:20 KJV). There is a power that works within us to bring whatever we think to pass. That power causes even the matters of the kings in our hearts can travel beyond the walls.

It Is Possible To Speak The Inner Tongue Without Opening Your Mouth

Many people speak in tongues in certain conditions where their mouths are not opened. Some release positive energy while others release negative energy. They say things in their heart that comes to pass positively or negatively. Words that are not rendered through the mouth can still develop a flying wing when rendered in the inner tongue. Unknown tongues can also be spoken like that. The ministry of angels can aid in carrying nonverbal words. Angels are like birds of the air carrying voices to the places of fulfillment. Hence, the scripture admonishes *"curse not the king, no not in thy thought; and curse not the rich in thy bedchamber: for a bird of the air shall carry the voice, and that which hath wings shall tell the matter" (Ecclesiastes 10:20 KJV).*

The words of the heart are usually objects before God. They can either be acceptable or non-acceptable. This is why the psalmist says *"Let the words of my mouth, and the meditation of my heart, be acceptable in thy sight, O Lord, my strength, and my redeemer" (Psalm 19:1 KJV).* God is a spirit. If those words are not naked before His spirit, then we would not have been instructed to guard our hearts with all diligence. The instruction to guard the heart tongue is more important because the heart is more dangerous *"Keep thy heart with all diligence; for out of it are the issues of life" (Proverbs 4:23).* You can speak in an unknown tongue using the inner tongue. This usually happens when people are in difficult situations or when they are just meditating. Those words uttered still fly with wings into places.

The Understanding Heart "A Knowing Tongue"

A knowing heart is a heart of understanding. It is the hearts that can control the tongue. This heart is powerful. It can discern tongues, intentions, and judgment at the same time. Words do come to such hearts without restraint. Even unknown tongues minister to hearts like that. I remember when the power of the Lord came upon a brother who fell down to start speaking in tongues, he said he had a tug in his heart saying something like a particular word echoing loudly and disturbing at the same time. It was asking him to speak out. This impression came to him through a knowing heart. The mouth usually knows what to say through a tug in the heart; the sign of a knowing heart even in the place of prayers.

Many people who usually speak in an unknown tongue do so dynamically because the

55

words they speak are usually like a bubbling river flowing from their hearts to their mouths. We know what to say when praying through the knowing heart. The understanding heart goes beyond talking, it can affect even judgment and perspective. The scripture says it this way: *"Give therefore thy servant an understanding heart to judge thy people, that I may discern between good and bad: for who is able to judge this thy so great a people?"(1 kings 3:9 KJV).* What this means is that a knowing heart will instruct his tongue, utterance, and perspective concerning issues relating to life. This is how a knowing heart can inform what we say when we speak in tongues.

The Vision of the Heart

The heart also can see a vision. This vision is different from that of the eyes. The eyes can be enlightened to see visions. These visions bring us into the state of knowing.

> *The eyes of your understanding being enlightened; that ye may know what is the hope of his calling, and what the riches of the glory of his inheritance in the saints"*
> *(Ephesians 1:18 KJV).*

There are two kinds of these visions:

1.   The God-inspired heart vision

This is the vision inspired by God. It is the God-birthed imagination of the heart. It can be a Holy Spirit-inspired imagination in the place of prayers. It comes to our minds from the spirit realm. This is where you see things that bring you to a greater level of knowing.

> *The eyes of your understanding being enlightened; that ye may know what is the hope of his calling, and what the riches of the glory of his inheritance in the saints"*
> *(Ephesians 1:18 KJV).*

2.   The vain vision of the heart

This is usually the imagination of one's heart. It comprises the selfish, defiling, and corrupt imagination of one's heart that violates the will of God. It is our responsibility to do away with them.

> *Thus saith the LORD of hosts, Hearken not unto the words of the prophets that prophesy unto you: they make you vain: they speak a vision of their own heart, and not out of the mouth of the LORD. They say still unto them that despise me, The LORD hath said, Ye*

shall have peace; and they say unto everyone that walketh after the imagination of his own heart, No evil shall come upon you"
(Jeremiah 23:16-17 KJV).

The Heart Tongue, the Dimension of Tongues for the Dumb

Speaking in peculiar tongues is possible at any level. It is a prophecy and promise of God for every one according to the word of God. This is the reason the dumb can be happy to know that it is possible to speak in tongues from the heart. The baptism of the Holy Spirit is for all with the exemption to no one. When we received the gift of speaking in tongues, it was the heart that got impacted with the gift before the mouth is being influenced . This is why we can switch operation to the mouth. Even the natural tongue was educated through the instruction of the heart by earthly educational institutions. The gift of speaking in tongues also educates the mind spiritually to yield to instruction physically . Therefore, the saints of God who are possibly in this condition of dumbness can participate in this experience after the following order :

1. Be baptised with the Holy Spirit
2. Desire the gift
3. Receive the gift to their hearts
4. Speak it in their hearts
5. Write it with their hands

Operating In This Dimension When Praying In Tongues

Everyone who prays in tongues has a key unbeknown to them. The best way to grow and experience this in your prayer life is to come to the knowledge of the requirement for operating in this dimension:

i. When praying, allow the Holy Spirit to flood your heart with unknown tongues. Usually, it happens like a flood of rivers surging through and flowing to the mouth.

ii. Do not be afraid to utter them when they are released to your heart and mouth. Sometimes, they sound first in your heart and then flow to your mouth.

iii. Be free to flow. Most people who are versatile in communicating in unknown tongues have the words mighty in their hearts like a force released into their hearts.

iv. Accept the faith that the spirit ministers to you during the occasion and for the occasion.

v. When the Holy Spirit reveals the names of people to your heart when praying, utter them.

vi. Give attention to the God-inspired imagination of your heart and not the vain drift.

vii. Pray the fresh and new tongues that God might reveal to your heart.

viii. Believe that God does speak to the heart, and the Holy Spirit can influence your heart with this evidence and gift in the place of prayers.

The Benefit of Operating in the Heart Tongue "A Knowing Heart"

There are a number of benefits of operating in this dimension:

i. It opens your heart to see things in the spirit.

ii. It helps you to connect with the spirit of the mystery words and the environment.

iii. It sharpens your discernment of good and bad.

iv. It sharpens your judgment.

v. It sharpens your spiritual perception.

Key Activation Prayers

Dear Holy Spirit, the fire and the power of God come upon me with your fresh power and in Jesus' name fill my heart with your fire so that I can begin to operate in this depth in Jesus' name. Amen!

Chapter

THE WRITING
DIMENSION OF TONGUES

CHAPTER SEVEN

THE WRITING DIMENSION OF TONGUES

"In the same hour came forth fingers of a man's hand, and wrote over against the candlestick upon the plaister of the wall of the king's palace: and the king saw the part of the hand that wrote" (Daniel 5:5 KJV).

It is possible to become a powerful person in your walk with God, such that when angels appear to you with written details you can be able to understand the writing and interpret it at the same time. As earlier said, knowledge is a vital tool for becoming one in the spirit. This is why this scripture makes that achievement a reality by providing the needed knowledge.

A recapitulation of what was said before in the previous chapter is that a set of written codes of instruction is usually seen as a language. Different kinds of languages can be identified through writing and not necessarily through speaking. Tongues can be written and can be spoken at the same time.

The order of writing in Heaven is far different from the earthly form. With many books being written in heaven to keep the account of creation, salvation and so on, one would imagine what angelic writing would look like if written on earth. However, an apt conclusion can be deduced that it would be undoubtedly different from that of a natural man. Elohim's power and government are a supreme code of His honor in every civilization. Whether in the spirit or human ecosystem, a clear boundary can be drawn as regards this. Here is a scriptural example:

"In the same hour came forth fingers of a man's hand, and wrote over against the candlestick upon the plaister of the wall of the king's palace: and the king saw the part of the hand that wrote. Then the king's countenance was changed, and his thoughts troubled him, so that the joints of his loins were loosed, and his knees smote one against another. The king cried aloud to bring in the astrologers, the Chaldeans, and the soothsayers. And the king spake, and said to the wise men of Babylon, Whosoever shall read this writing, and shew me the interpretation thereof, shall be clothed with scarlet, and have a chain of gold about his neck, and shall be the third ruler in the kingdom.

*Then came in all the king's wise men: but they could not read the writing, nor make
known to the king the interpretation thereof"
(Daniel 5: 5-8 KJV).*

*"And thou his son, O Belshazzar, hast not humbled thine heart, though thou knewest all this;
But hast lifted up thyself against the Lord of heaven; and they have brought the vessels of his
house before thee, and thou, and thy lords, thy wives, and thy concubines, have drunk wine in
them; and thou hast praised the gods of silver, and gold, of brass, iron, wood, and stone,
which see not, nor hear, nor know: and the God in whose hand thy breath is, and whose are
all thy ways, hast thou not glorified:*

*Then was the part of the hand sent from him; and this writing was written. And this is the
writing that was written, Mene, Mene, Tekel, Upharsin. This is the interpretation of the
thing: Mene; God hath numbered thy kingdom, and finished it. Tekel; Thou art weighed
in the balances, and art found wanting. Peres; Thy kingdom is divided,
and given to the Medes and Persians" (Daniel 5:22-28 KJV).*

No doubt, what was written is the tongue of angels! The words spoken are *"Mene, Mene,
Tekel, Upharsin "*. These words have no recorded meaning anywhere in the world or in any
history of the world. Only Daniel was able to interpret the tongue of the angel written on the
wall. Daniel was said to be a distinct man at that age. The amplitude of his knowledge went
beyond the realm of a mortal man. No match reference was given to any other personality on
earth in his days. The accolade says:

*"There is a man in thy kingdom, in whom is the spirit of
the holy gods; and in the days of thy father light and
understanding and wisdom, like the wisdom of the gods,
was found in him; whom the king Nebuchadnezzar thy
father, the king, I say, thy father, made master of the
magicians, astrologers, Chaldeans, and soothsayers"
(Daniel 5:11 KJV).*

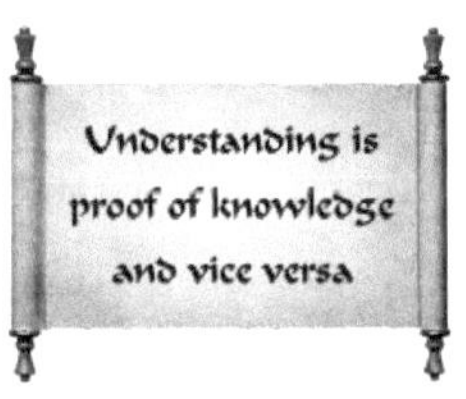

Know this; understanding is proof of knowledge and vice versa. No man can interpret an
unfamiliar tongue. Daniel's ability to interpret the tongue of the angel is nothing but a
testament that he spoke the language of the spirit and that he somewhat had spiritual acumen
of it. Daniel was the first man to interpret tongues in the Bible. He was nothing but a spiritual

juggernaut for being able to peep into heaven and have an idea of a barricaded language.

Diverse angels can communicate with different angelic writings. Some of these writings can be earthly or spiritual. However, each chosen mode of communication is always dependent on the nature of the assignment, the intention of God, the communication cycle, and the receiver. Hence, every communication pathway between angels and man is well-protected and monitored by God.

This will make me say whenever we want to quote this scripture *"Though I speak with the tongues of men and of angels, and have not charity, I am become as sounding brass, or a tinkling cymbal" (1 Corinthians 13:1 KJV)*, we should put the fact that angels can also speak the tongues of men into consideration.

Understanding Angelic Writings

Day by day, the immortals bid us with writings. Sometimes, these angels know that we are not so familiar with their realms so they give us more than enough signs for us to be able to grasp their communications. There are three major things we will discuss now as the pivots to knowing and understanding angelic writings:

i.   Displayed letters of angels

Letters can be displayed for the sake of communication. Sometimes it can be a whole sentence and at some other times, it might be flashes and displays of letters. In the case where letters are being displayed one needs to be very sensitive to picking all the details of the information. Just like the case below:

> *"Then was the part of the hand sent from him; and this writing was written. And this is the writing that was written, Mene, Mene, Tekel, Upharsin. This is the interpretation of the thing: Mene; God hath numbered thy kingdom, and finished it. Tekel; Thou art weighed in the balances, and art found wanting. Peres; Thy kingdom is divided, and given to the Medes and Persians" (Daniel 5:22-28 KJV).*

This was a full sentence written in the tongue of angels. Sometimes, it can be a display of letters one after the other where the one involved might have to interpret and also put the letters together to facilitate understanding.

ii.   Shape and Symbol Signs of angels

Shapes, symbols, and signs are also being used as a mode of communication. For instance, auditory, visual, and tactile modes can be used to communicate with those who are deaf-blind physically. Common visual communication includes cued speech, speech or lip reading, gestures, and sign language which are also being used for deaf-blind people. All of these can be used in communication but it depends on whom the communication has to do with. This is the reason angels can talk and write to us differently.

Shape and symbol signs have been used to denote many road signs, especially on our highways and busy roads for the purpose of regulatory measures, guide, informative and directive measures as well as warning signs. These signs range from caution signs, warning signs, safety signs, driving signs, traffic rules, highway signs, street signs, speed limits, and so on.

iii.   Color Displays of angels

Angels do write with colors and symbols in the atmosphere. They can display these to pass their messages. These angelic writings can be likened in purpose to the usage of a traffic light in controlling traffic. Using this to adumbrate our objectives in this way will surely cause you to learn a great deal. The traffic light consists of three lights; red, yellow, and green. The red means stop, the yellow means slow down and wait and the green means go. These are being used to guide drivers. On the other hand, yellow with black lettering or symbols with diamond shapes are signs of warning telling you to slow down and stop if necessary; a special situation or hazard may be on the way or ahead. This is exactly how many of us do receive angelic writing for our guidance.

In addition, we cannot overemphasize the fact that angelic writings are impressions and imprints of angels on nature for the purpose of communication. These impressions can be color codes. They can be in handwriting, shapes, and forms. Sometimes, the writings are usually ambiguous, because the angels are not from this realm. It can also be a deliberate attempt to push the receiver to a realm of deeper inquiry through access to a tip of information.

The Writing Tongue Is A Branch Of Vision Tongue

We will elaborate more about vision tongue in the next chapter. The spiritual mechanism powering the writing dimension is vision even though it can be physical at many times. The reality of the vision scape or physical sight is dependent on God and the purpose for which

He sends His messenger angel. However, if you look at the experience of the king in the days of Daniel according to the scriptures:

"In the same hour came forth fingers of a man's hand, and wrote over against the candlestick upon the plaister of the wall of the king's palace: and the king saw the part of the hand that wrote" (Daniel 5:22-28 KJV). The king saw the writing. He called many people to come and see it, and they all saw it. It was a public message for the whole kingdom and the reign of the king.

What to know about this writing dimension:
i.   It can be spoken when praying as it can be stumbled upon, seen, and spoken without paying attention.
ii.   It can be seen by everyone in most cases if it is a public message.
iii.   It can be letters, names of people, and numbers.
iv.   It can be seen.
v.   It can be a given message or word in form of human understanding.
vi.   It can be familiar and unfamiliar words in form of visions or physical letters in many cases.

The Ecological Community for Experiencing Angelic Writings

Over the years, there have been a lot of testimonies recorded in different parts of the world about angelic writings. Some of them have seen writings on trees, clouds, animals, stones, and babies.

These angelic writings do pose an undying passion for spiritual inquiries about one's immediate environment. They are sometimes in figures and forms. They can be in the display of numbers or letters. The purpose once again is communication. There are two ecosystems where angelic writings can be experienced by an individual or a group of people:

i.   Physical domain: image and figures, houses, human body, objects, environment, clouds, and so on.

An angel can write physically on objects like houses, clouds, animals, and so on. We can see these writing in different ways like in figures, images, and handwriting. They can be whole and physical. They can be on car surfaces and anything around us even on a human forehead. Some examples will be highlighted below:

The Writing On The Wall

This is like the king's experience in his palace. In his case, he saw a hand writing over against the candlestick upon the plaister of the wall of the palace. Since He was born, he had never had such an experience before.

"In the same hour came forth fingers of a man's hand, and wrote over against the candlestick upon the plaister of the wall of the king's palace: and the king saw the part of the hand that wrote. Then the king's countenance was changed, and his thoughts troubled him, so that the joints of his loins were loosed, and his knees smote one against another. The king cried aloud to bring in the astrologers, the Chaldeans, and the soothsayers. And the king spake, and said to the wise men of Babylon, whosoever shall read this writing, and shew me the interpretation thereof, shall be clothed with scarlet, and have a chain of gold about his neck, and shall be the third ruler in the kingdom. Then came in all the king's wise men: but they could not read the writing, nor make known to the king the interpretation thereof" (Daniel 5: 5-8 KJV).

This scripture lets you know that it is possible for an angel to write on walls.

The Hand In The Cloud "The Figure Writing"

The hand-in-the-cloud illustration is nothing but a glimpse of spiritual consecution and assertions through the bible that one can actually keep up with timely divine messages in our present-day world by the mere understanding of certain spiritual revelations. The Lord is always speaking to us but not too many people can hear or decode the means through which He is speaking.

There was a need for rain during the time of Elijah. The man of God who was trusting for a sign that God has heard him. Only one proof will be needed to know that God has heard. It will be a cloud formation. The man of God asked the servant to go look toward the sea. Whatever he sees would measure up with what Elijah has heard and has been expecting. Let us look at the hand that was formed in the cloud in response as an answer to his prayers. What does it represent? The hand was simply saying something but the servant of Elijah heard no voice. He only saw a cloud like the hand of a man.

"And said to his servant, Go up now, look toward the sea. And he went up, and looked, and said, there is nothing. And he said, Go again seven times. And it came to pass at the seventh time, that he said, Behold, there ariseth a little cloud out of the sea, like a man's hand. And he said, Go up, say unto Ahab, Prepare thy chariot, and get thee down that

the rain stop thee not. And it came to pass in the meanwhile, that the heaven was black with clouds and wind, and there was a great rain. And Ahab rode, and went to Jezreel" (1 kings 18:43-45).

Do you know that it was the hand that gathered the cloud? It was the same hand that came upon Elijah to overtake Ahab's chariots of horses with bare feet.

"And the hand of the Lord was on Elijah; and he girded up his loins, and ran before Ahab to the entrance of Jezreel" (1 kings 18:43-45). It did not take time for the rain cloud to fill everywhere. The rain took over everywhere with speed just as Elijah was given speed on his feet.

Recurrently, God does show us the writing in this manner but not many do understand them, the reason being that the writing doesn't usually come with voices.

ii. *The Spirit Realm; (Visions And Dreams):* The spirit realm is also a good avenue to experience angelic writing. They are sometimes seen in the spirit realm in form of visions, dreams, and so on. Angelic writings don't just pose themselves as a human form of writings all the time. They do exist to inform us of impressions and imprints for the purpose of human-to-spirit communications and spirit-to-human communications.

They are expressed to give interpretations and understanding. The range of angelic writing appearances is from letters, shapes, and colors to physical and spiritual numbers even in form of visions. Some have had to experience them in form of a cloud shape, burning fire impressions, images, and many others. The same experience of the king can be an experience in a vision. Just the way it is written in the scripture:

"In the same hour came forth fingers of a man's hand, and wrote over against the candlestick upon the plaister of the wall of the king's palace: and the king saw the part of the hand that wrote. Then the king's countenance was changed, and his thoughts troubled him, so that the joints of his loins were loosed, and his knees smote one against another. The king cried aloud to bring in the astrologers, the Chaldeans, and the soothsayers. And the king spake, and said to the wise men of Babylon, whosoever shall read this writing, and shew me the interpretation thereof, shall be clothed with scarlet, and have a chain of gold about his neck, and shall be the third ruler in the kingdom. Then came in all the king's wise men: but they could not read the writing, nor make

known to the king the interpretation thereof"
(Daniel 5: 5-8 KJV).

A dream can also produce such writing: The vision of the night can be so detailed that a whole future can be captured within the revelation as this or even more. It is possible for one to have this experience in another realm of visions. Moses also hosted an angel of the Lord in form of fire. The scripture says:

"There the angel of the Lord appeared to him in flames of fire from within a bush. Moses saw that though the bush was on fire it did not burn up" (Exodus 3:2 NIV). The voice that accompanied the vision is what gave understanding to the revelation of Moses. Many at times, there may not be a voice and we may have to decode the voice ourselves.

There are so many people who have hosted angels like this. Some have seen this in the place of prayers. When they began to pray some saw fire. They never knew what the fire represented. The fire they saw could have meant an angel. This is why we need to know and learn about angelic writing.

The Writing Dimension of Tongues, the Dimension of Tongues for the Dumb and Deaf Saints or Those Who Lost Their Speech Organ.

Again, going by the revelation that the baptism of the Holy Spirit is for all with the exemption to no one and that when we received the gift of speaking in tongues, it was the heart that got impacted with the gift before the mouth is being influenced, hence, fellow saints of God who are either deaf and dumb can engage the writing dimension . As said above, the natural tongue was educated through the instruction of the heart by earthly educational institutions. Same order can be followed as in the heart dimension :

1. Be baptised with the Holy Spirit
2. Desire the gift
3. Receive the gift to their hearts
4. Speak it in their hearts
5. Write it with their fingers or pen as the Holy Spirit gives utterance

Zechariah from the book of Luke chapter 1 could be likened to anyone who lost speech organ or was deaf or dumb at a time. Zechariah lost speech but engaged writing because his heart was not deformed or devoid of the past encounter . Although Zechariah did not speak in tongues at the time because Jesus Christ was not yet on earth let alone glorified through His death. However, just imagine if it was a believer who has the gift of speaking in tongues that lost his speech, what do you think will happen to his gift of speaking in tongues , and what will happen again if he regains his speech? This should inform anyone that it is the heart that is impacted to influence the tongue. The writing dimension of tongues is possible.

Daniel's Tips to Operating in the Writing Dimension of Speaking In Tongues

The many-sided wisdom of God has helped man to really come to a place where what is spoken can be written, and understood. We can be instructed in the place of prayers by angels or by God to say certain things. This brings to mind the fact that our fellowship in the place of prayers should be mutual with God. We talk to Him and He talks back to us. Using the analogy of the king's experience, we can deduce so many things and these will lead us to understand the way to function in the place of prayer:

I.   The writing was a symbol upon a branch of fire "the candle stick ": *"In the same hour came forth fingers of a man's hand, and wrote over against the candlestick upon the plaister of the wall of the king's palace: and the king saw the part of the hand that wrote ".*

ii.   The language or the tongue written by the angel has never been spoken before in all the realms of the king's reign and powers whether present or past and in the history of men at this time:

iii.   *"In the same hour came forth fingers of a man's hand, and wrote over against the candlestick upon the plaister of the wall of the king's palace: and the king saw the part of the hand that wrote. Then the king's countenance was changed, and his thoughts troubled him, so that the joints of his loins were loosed, and his knees smote one against another. The king cried aloud to bring in the astrologers, the Chaldeans, and the soothsayers. And the king spake, and said to the wise men of Babylon, whosoever shall read this writing, and shew me the interpretation thereof, shall be clothed with scarlet, and have a chain of gold about his neck, and shall be the third ruler in the kingdom. Then came in all the king's wise men: but they could not read the writing, nor make known to the king the interpretation thereof"(Daniel 5: 5-8 KJV).*

No history has ever captured this tongue not even the demonic world at this time. It seemed this was the first time the Lord would be introducing it to the earthly realm.

iii. The interpretation would require the wisdom, knowledge, and the spirit of the Holy Gods.

"There is a man in thy kingdom, in whom is the spirit of the holy gods; and in the days of thy father light and understanding and wisdom, like the wisdom of the gods, was found in him; whom the king Nebuchadnezzar thy father, the king, I say, thy father, made master of the magicians, astrologers, Chaldeans, and soothsayers" (Daniel 5:11 KJV).

No one could fault the interpretation of Daniel because no one in the world knew what the writing was all about. Only by manifestation would they be able to prove what was said to be either relevant or irrelevant.

iv. Daniel was the first man to speak in an unknown tongue through interpretation. No one in history could interpret the tongue they could not speak. Understanding precedes speaking and interpretation:

"Then was the part of the hand sent from him; and this writing was written. And this is the writing that was written, Mene, Mene, Tekel, Upharsin. This is the interpretation of the thing: Mene; God hath numbered thy kingdom, and finished it. Tekel; Thou art weighed in the balances, and art found wanting. Peres; Thy kingdom is divided, and given to the Medes and Persians" (Daniel 5:22-28 KJV).

v. Divine messages can be written and given to us in foreign tongues:

The angel who wrote those words knew that the man was not familiar with them. Yet he wrote it. When we pray, we can be made to see and speak words like this.

vi. Let your understanding be connected to receiving feedback: In the place of prayers, the writing can be in understanding, and in some cases, it may be in an unknown tongue. Many people can just see names fly in the place of prayers like that.

vii. Opening our hearts to God in the place of prayers can be a good way to operate in the writing dimension. When one sees such writing, there is a need for vision to understand the writing. This is why the Bible says in the New Testament:

"That the God of our Lord Jesus Christ, the Father of glory, may give to you the spirit of wisdom and revelation in the knowledge of Him, the eyes of your understanding

being enlightened; that you may know what is the hope of His calling, what are the riches of the glory of His inheritance in the saints" (Ephesian 1:17-18 NKJV).

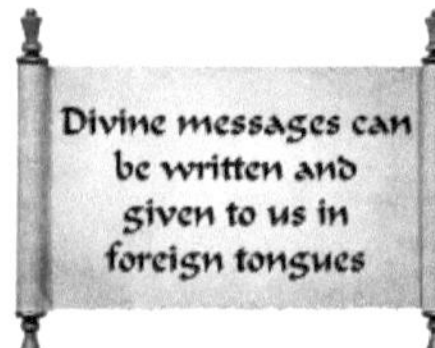

For instance, an angel's hand can just be writing like that in the place of prayers. Physically one can see an angel write numbers and names on walls. This may not happen every time but it can happen at many times. The exceptional thing about the writing dimension of tongue is that it can be both physical and spiritual in experience. There is a slight difference from the vision dimension. On some occasions, everyone can see the writing just as the astrologers, and magicians, and everyone saw the one in the days of Daniel. It can be personal in the place of prayer or general if it is a public message.

Key Activation Prayers

Awesome Holy Spirit, come upon me with your fresh power and anointing, fill me afresh with this dimension. Impact my spiritual sense with the ability to enjoy this reality now in Jesus' name. Amen!

Chapter

THE VISION DIMENSION
OF TONGUES

CHAPTER EIGHT

THE VISION DIMENSION OF TONGUES

"In the same hour came forth fingers of a man's hand, and wrote over against the candlestick upon the plaster of the wall of the king's palace: and the king saw the part of the hand that wrote" (Daniel 5:5 KJV).

There is a visual dimension of tongues that reveals the expressed voice of God. When one comes into it, a greater level of confidence and understanding in a relationship with the divine is introduced. It is always an exciting thing to explore this dimension. Vision-tongues are revelational. They don't come through mechanical modes of speaking in tongues. Spiritual tongues can propel visions, and visions can propel tongues. The apostle's tongues were first received as visions before they were spoken. This is what brought light to my spirit that an unknown tongue can be written, seen as a vision, and then spoken. This is how to prepare yourself for praying in tongues in the senior class. Let us see the tips of the apostle's tongues:

"They saw what seemed to be tongues of fire that separated and came to rest on each of them" (Acts 2:3 NIV).

How does one see what seemed like a tongue and start speaking what they saw? This is the description of what the Apostles experienced as shown in the scripture above. The Apostles saw the vision of the tongues inform of signs of fire and then spoke what they saw. Isn't that powerful to know that tongues can be seen? This blew my mind! I read it again and again. They saw tongues! Hence, I said to myself, it is possible for me to see my tongue too. What I speak can be seen! Then I remember that Daniel only saw but he got interpretation from the spirit realm through the wisdom of the Holy God. This has helped me to see the writing of tongues before I speak many times. I see tongues written and then I speak it.

What They Saw is What They Spoke "The How of Operation"

The description of what the disciples saw was like an emblem of fire. What they saw divided itself upon many of them and they began to act alike. How I wish our tongue-speaking experience can always be like this! First a vision and then an influence.

My recent observation is that it is possible for all believers to see their tongues. However, they are not always aware of it, neither are they prepared for it. Most of the time, the believers' tongues come from already registered mental pictures, a predetermined mode of speaking; a pattern readily engraved in the heart of the people instead of a regular vision of divine utterance. For instance, you'll hear many believers say "goyi goyi" for many years; something they have kept in their hearts; usually unchanging and uninteresting. Rather than tongues becoming a vision or a revelation in their hearts and a fresh utterance of fire, they go about saying "hello, hello" for many years thinking it will mean many things in the spirit. God is a spirit and we have seen Him speak in the spirit to many saints He spoke expressly to Jesus *This is my beloved Son in whom I am well pleased"* (Mathew 3:17 KJV). Two words could not have communicated more thoughts in God's heart than the many words, else He would have spoken two words alone and might not have communicated His mind.

Also, I do have observations. My observations in a few years might help some people to retrace their steps from making mistakes when it comes to speaking in tongues. Below listed are the three observations:

i.   Didactic and Mechanical tongues": They are three distinct modes of speaking in tongues that have to do with;

    a.   The teacher's instructions in the form of teaching before laying of hands for the impartation of the pure gift.
    b.   The teacher who does not teach but asks people to say for instance "bla bla".
    c.   An individual age-long unchanging repetitive single line of tongues.

The first one is the teacher who teaches you from the scripture about the importance of tongues and then imparts you with the gift. Secondly, the teacher who teaches someone how to speak "blabla". This second part is usually very wrong. You don't need to teach anyone "blabla" to be able to speak in tongues. Better to follow the former and neglect the latter. The third one is due to the ignorance of an individual and perhaps the unwillingness of the individual to learn the word, open their spirit to God and allow him to flood their hearts with the inspiration.

ii.   Drop and pick tongues "the Stolen tongues": These are people's refurbished tongues. They are types of spoken tongues copied by others. Tongues even though they are mysteries do have meaning when being interpreted. Going about picking tongues without knowing the interpretation of what it means might not be too good. I am not talking about rhythm but words. There are demonic utterances also in the form of tongues. Even in the good one, what if the person is saying things like "Oh God I am a murderer, I killed many people please have mercy on me". Some steal tongues from others without asking for the interpretation of the stolen words. Well, stolen tongues if interpreted might be edifying else it will be like the one who is calling himself a thief in an unfamiliar tongue. However, what God says in the scripture might give an idea of what stance to take:

"Therefore behold, I am against the prophets," saith the Lord,
"that steal My words every one from his neighbor"
(Jeremiah 23:30)

iii.   Revelational Tongues: They are autodidactic in nature. They are directly from the throne. They are self-instructive.

Channels Of The Vision Dimension Of Tongues

There are organs of the spirit that can be influenced to see visions. These are the Heart of Man, spiritual eyes, and physical eyes. The enlightenment and the opening of these cavities to the spirit realm means access to visions. The information shared in this book is interconnected. Reading other chapters will enlighten you about the previous chapters. However, we will talk about the physical eyes and the enlightened heart.

The disciples of Jesus saw the vision tongue. All of them saw it. It was real.

"They saw what seemed to be tongues of fire that separated and came to rest on each of them" (Acts 2:3 NIV).

1.   The Physical Eyes:
There are visions that do not require physical eyes. However, the physical eye is access to real encounter vision. Gideon's case is a good example:

"And there came an angel of the LORD, and sat under an oak which was in Ophrah, that pertained unto Joash the Abiezrite: and his son Gideon threshed wheat by the winepress, to hide it from the Midianites. And the angel of the LORD appeared unto him, and said unto him, The LORD is with thee, thou mighty man of valour. And Gideon said unto him, Oh my Lord, if the LORD be with us, why then is all this befallen us? and where be all his miracles which our fathers told us of, saying, Did not the LORD bring us up from Egypt? but now the LORD hath forsaken us, and delivered us into the hands of the Midianites" (Judges 6:11-13 KJV).

Tongues can be captured with physical eyes. The way the angel sat can just be the way tongues can be written physically and captured. I have seen stuffs and letters like that with the physical eyes.

2.   The spiritual eyes

This usually has to do with the eyes of the spirit or the mind and heart in some cases.

"And he said, I saw all Israel scattered upon the hills, as sheep that have not a shepherd: and the LORD said, These have no master: let them return every man to his house in peace" (1 kings 22:17 KJV).

Micaiah's vision was never inspired physically. It was not an imagination it was a vision. He saw things in the spirit. He saw the future. This is also how one can see tongues in the spirit. It can be with spiritual eyes.

3.   The heart of man

Man's heart can work in an imaginative form. When your heart is enlightened visions can be captured. Tongues also can be captured.

"The eyes of your understanding being enlightened; that ye may know what is the hope of his calling, and what the riches of the glory of his inheritance in the saints (Ephesians 1:18 KJV).

First A Vision and Then an Influence

The fantastic thing about the unknown tongue being a vision before an influence is that everyone that receives tongues as visions received the accompanying energy to pray it without asking for any sign to move further. *They saw what seemed to be tongues of fire that separated and came to rest on each of them (Acts 2:3 NIV).* What they saw in the vision according to the scripture came with the power of influence. There was no moment to think of what to do with what they saw. The fire and the energy of what they saw came upon them. The activation of tongues and the resemblance of tongues in visions are like:

i.   A symbol of the tongue with Fire

This means holy tongue shape symbols that appear while praying. It can be once or throughout the prayer session. Sometimes, it might be saying something and then influencing the one praying to pray in His direction. It might just be a tongue sign of the fire that came to rest on the fellow praying. The apostles saw it once and it rested on them for operations. Diverse people still experience it the same way today. It usually comes with a resting influence. It brings freshness to the place of prayer. It discourages premeditated tongues and opens the portal of immediate connection with divinity.

ii.   Tongues presented in letters

This takes us back to the writing dimension of tongues. It is the situation in which one speaks the letters he is seeing in a visual array.

iii.   Tongues presented in form of figures

These are fire symbols presented in form of numbers. They can reveal things in the spirit especially when they are being engaged in prayers.

iv.   Tongues presented with other symbols

Tongues can be presented with other symbols. These can include shapes and significant elements.

v.   Tongues presented in form of images

Tongues can unveil images. Most of the images might be part of the things in the discussion in the spirit. Images of known people, angels that are part of the prayer negotiations, cities, nations, and so on. The reason for this is because communication in tongues even though they are mysteries, they do have so much to do with the affairs of life and the matters of this world and the world to come.

All of these being spiritual examples are just also typical illustrations of how humans learn how to communicate in the physical. In many schools in Africa, the elementary classes, an image is attached to a letter as well as shapes are attached to names and identities for communication and learning. Whenever one is praying and these are seen, there is usually a push to say something and pray in the direction of what is seen.

Operating in the vision dimension of Tongues

In an environment where one prays in understanding, in an unknown tongue or in the spirit, it is possible to burst into the realms of the vision dimension of tongues unconsciously. Most times, people do see names of people, houses, some old friends, and many more. It begins to look like their imagination is becoming active. They begin to pray about what they are seeing, calling those things by names. This is no exemption to whether they are praying in

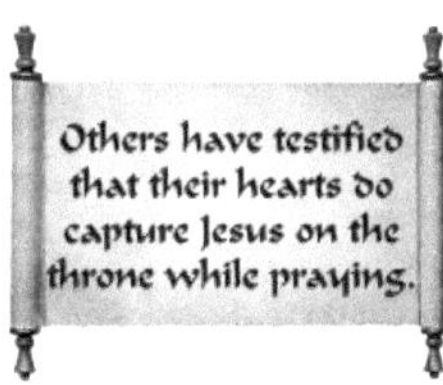

tongues or in understanding. During prayer, many people have affirmed seeing a different thing, some experienced negative visions which might be an attempt from the enemy to destroy their plans during prayer, while others do get positive images of different things, thinking it is just their thoughts. These are nothing but tongue visions activated through prayers and heart concentration on intercession. Others have testified that their hearts do capture Jesus on the throne while praying. This is the perfect description of the Holy Ghost sojourning. The revelation of tongue vision is an operation of the Holy Spirit.

"Now there are diversities of gifts, but the same Spirit" (1 Corinthians 12:4 KJV)

It can capture words with interpretation, mystery tongue declaration, audible pronunciation of words, images, angels talking, God declaring, the vision of fire emblem, and so on. This is the complexity of its diversity in operation. How then can one successfully operate in the vision dimension of tongues? Below are a few answers:

i.   The baptism of the Holy Ghost: This is the person who ushers in the great experience. He is the beginning of vision enablement. *"They saw what seemed to be tongues of fire that separated and came to rest on each of them" (Acts 2:3 NIV).*

ii.   The continuous infilling of the Holy Spirit:
"Do not get drunk with wine, for that is wickedness (corruption, stupidity), but be filled with the [Holy] Spirit and constantly guided by Him" (Ephesians 5:18 AMP).

iii.   Pray for the baptism of the vision gift from the Holy Spirit:
"Now there are diversities of gifts, but the same Spirit. And there are differences of administrations, but the same Lord. And there are diversities of operations, but it is the same God which worketh all in all. But the manifestation of the Spirit is given to every man to

profit withal. For to one is given by the Spirit the word of wisdom; to another the word of knowledge by the same Spirit" (1 Corinthians 12:4-8 KJV).

iv.   Purify yourself from the filthiness of the spirit:
Create in me a clean heart, O God; and renew a right spirit within me (Psalm 51:10 KJV).

v.   Cleanse yourself from the filthiness of the flesh:

"Having, therefore, these promises, dearly beloved, let us cleanse ourselves from all filthiness of the flesh and spirit, perfecting holiness in the fear of God"
(2 Corinthians 7:1 KJV).

vi.   Pray that the eyes of your understanding will be enlightened:
"That the God of our Lord Jesus Christ, the Father of glory, may give unto you the spirit of wisdom and revelation in the knowledge of him: The eyes of your understanding being enlightened; that ye may know what is the hope of his calling, and what the riches of the glory of his inheritance in the saints"
(Ephesians 1:17-18 KJV).

vii.   Be open-hearted in the place of prayer.
vii.   Be sensitive to the push and move of the Holy Spirit in the place of prayers.
ix.   Don't be rigid when you are directed by the Holy Spirit:

For as many as are led by the Spirit of God, they are the sons of God (Romans 8:14 KJV).

Differentiate The Thin Line

The tongue vision dimension is a revelation from the Lord that can engage your physical organs such as eyes, ears, tongues, hearts, and minds. However, we need to know that there are also vain visions that can also be in the hearts of men. They are usually not pioneered by the spirit of God but by self or demons. Take for instance when you begin to imagine negative things in the place of prayers, becoming distracted from praying. This could be a move from the vainness of your heart or an interaction with a demon. We must be very sure of who is pioneering our vision:

"But strong meat belongeth to them that are of full age, even those who by reason of use have their senses exercised to discern both good and evil" (Hebrews 5:14 KJV).

The more we use our spiritual senses the more we become mature. We need to be careful with an empty vision: *Thus says the Lord of hosts, "Do not listen to the words of the [false] prophets who prophesy to you. They are teaching you worthless things and are leading you into futility; they speak a vision of their own mind and imagination and not [truth] from the mouth of the Lord (Jeremiah 23:16 AMP).*

Key Activation Prayers

Holy Spirit come upon me with your fresh power and anointing. Release your fire upon me. Activate the vision dimension of tongue. Cause me to function with understanding. Help me not to be deceived by the devil as I operate in this reality in Jesus name. Amen!

Chapter

9

THE OPEN DIMENSION
OF TONGUES

CHAPTER NINE

THE OPEN DIMENSION OF TONGUES

"I am the Lord thy God, which brought thee out of the land of Egypt: open thy mouth wide and I will fill it." (Psalm 81:10 KJV).

This dimension is known for the express will of the Spirit in utterance. The Lord seldomly fills the mouth of the saints who walk in this dimension with impeccable words. He gives them utterances for effective spiritual communication. The Spirit urges them in every way to communicate His mind whether with understandable words or in an unknown tongue. He does the pushing and the talking at the same time. The energy and the revelation of this kind of prayer usually come from Him. It is an act that is based on His timing; His hours. The opening of the mouth could be done in Spirit in form of unknown tongues or understanding. The Spirit expresses concerns by Himself. This is not "I have so many things to say kind of prayer but He (the Spirit) has so many things to tell God for me.

"But when they deliver you up, take no thought how or what ye shall speak: for it shall be given you in that same hour what ye shall speak. For it is not ye that speak, but the Spirit of your Father which speaketh in you" (Mathew 10:19-20 KJV).

The cardinal word in the above is the same as the major pivot for this dimension *"the spirit of your father which speaketh in you"*. Once a believer receives the Holy Ghost, He's got an opportunity to be led by the spirit. This is the spirit of faith. Even if he has not received the gift of speaking in tongues, his words can be guided by the Holy Spirit The requirement for this dimension is that one must be born again but not necessarily have received the gift of speaking in tongues. The Spirit of faith in the fellow is the one that unleashes the impeccable word in tandem with faith from the mouth of the individual.

Moreover, in this dimension, the one speaking words or praying in an unknown tongue mostly receives a tug in the spirit to say things they never intended to say. They may not possibly hear the words. The Holy Spirit just fills their mouths with the words. They just say it, just knowing what to say. In many cases, they may not even know that they are the ones who said those words until it has come out. This then takes us closer to the consciousness of the open dimension of tongues. What should its consciousness be like? Anyone who must be ready to operate in this consciousness must be ready to uphold:

i.   Faith without compromise

Faith is the factor that helps you act on the word of God. It is the same factor that helps you speak when the Holy Ghost is giving you the urge of the open dimension. No resistance will be permitted through faith "*But without faith, it is impossible to please him: for he that cometh to God must believe that he is, and that he is a rewarder of them that diligently seek him" (Hebrews 11:6 KJV).* Faith is the only weapon that can help believers never to be destroyed in the face of strong opposition. At these times, the open dimension may need to find expression because the heart of man is troubled by not knowing what to pray for. Hence, the Spirit of God renders prayers for a man with specific pertinent words, as man opens his mouth in prayers.

"Holding faith, and a good conscience; which some having put away concerning faith have made shipwreck" (1 Timothy 1:19 KJV).

ii.   A pure Conscience

The mystery of a pure conscience is that it helps to oust doubts from the heart. It gets rid of evil with any contemplation. It never allows sorrow and evil to sit in the faculty of the soul or spirit.

"Holding the mystery of the faith in a pure conscience" (1 Timothy 3:9 KJV).

iii.   The word of faith

God's word is a weapon of the Holy Spirit for addressing diverse situations. It has the capacity to affect human intelligence. It is so immaculate that it can address whatever it is being directed at. It is called the word of faith in our mouths:

"But what saith it? The word is nigh thee, even in thy mouth, and in thy heart: that is, the word of faith, which we preach" (Romans 10:8 KJV).

It is the best mission agent. In all situations, it does not fail.

"For as the rain cometh down, and the snow from heaven, and returneth not thither, but watereth the earth, and maketh it bring forth and bud, that it may give seed to the sower, and bread to the eater: So shall my word be that goeth forth out of my mouth: it shall not

return unto me void, but it shall accomplish that which I please, and it shall prosper in the thing whereto I sent it" (Isaiah 55:10-11 KJV).

iv.   Trust in the leading of the Holy Spirit

The regenerated spirit of man joined with the Holy Spirit is a good guide in the situations of life. According to the scriptures:

"The spirit of man is the candle of the Lord, searching all the inward parts of the belly" (Proverbs 20:27 KJV).

v.   A bridled-tongue mindset

A deliberate attempt has to be made to maintain this consciousness. It starts with being slow to speak but quick to listen:

"Wherefore, my beloved brethren, let every man be swift to hear, slow to speak, slow to wrath" (James 1:19 KJV).
"For in many things we offend all. If any man offends not in word, the same is a perfect man, and able also to bridle the whole body" (James 3:2 KJV).

vi.   The right association

Do away with the wrong association. Even if the Holy Spirit has so much to say, He will be doubted and resisted in the company of a doubting group.

"Be not deceived: evil communications corrupt good manners" (1 Corinthians 15:33 KJV).

The good-mannered recommendation of the spirit can be doubted and thwarted in the face of a doubting company. On the other hand, a good company can help the Holy Ghost leap like a baby in the womb of a pregnant woman concerning the good matter. It gives light and expression to the voice of God in the face of a daunting challenge. Such was the case of the three Hebrew brothers. The Holy Ghost gave them words. They operated in the open dimension of tongues. It was not an unknown tongue but the native tongue of understanding. When they spoke, it was the Spirit of God speaking through them. What they affirmed happened as they were rescued from a furnace of fire:

"Shadrach, Meshach, and Abednego answered and said to the king, O Nebuchadnezzar, we are not careful to answer thee in this matter. If it be so, our God whom we serve is able to deliver us from the burning fiery furnace, and he will deliver us out of thine hand, O king. But if not, be it known unto thee, O king, that we will not serve thy gods, nor worship the golden image which thou hast set up" (Daniel 3: 16-18 KJV).

vii.   Communion with God

Constant fellowship with God causes increased grace to abide with us at all times for all experiences. This is how we service our spirit for the open dimension of tongues.

"Brethren, the grace of our Lord Jesus Christ be with your spirit. Amen.
"(Galatians 6:18 KJV).

viii. A guarded heart

One major factor that is needed to operate in this dimension is a heart that is constantly guarded against contamination of the world. If your heart can easily be troubled, it may be difficult to operate in this dimension. You will easily be dismayed.

Let your heart be still, and protected from contamination. This is all about the fixing of the heart on God:

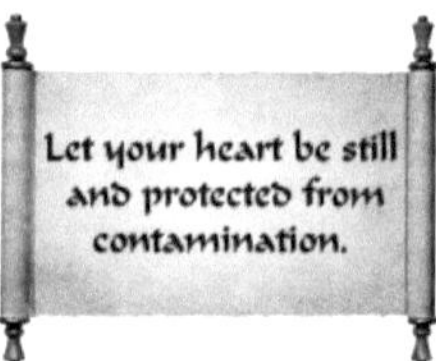

"My heart is fixed, O God, my heart is fixed: I will sing and give praise" (Psalm 57:7 KJV).
"Thou wilt keep him in perfect peace, whose mind is stayed on thee: because he trusteth in thee "(Isaiah 26:3 KJV).
This is the way you can experience stillness at all times and restoration in the face of threat. It will make you never fear any evil in the valley of the shadow of death, and you can comfortably host a dinner in the face of your enemies.

"He maketh me to lie down in green pastures: he leadeth me beside the still waters. He restoreth my soul: he leadeth me in the paths of righteousness for his name's sake. Yea, though I walk through the valley of the shadow of death, I will fear no evil: for thou art with me; thy rod and thy staff they comfort me. Thou preparest a table before me in the presence of mine enemies: thou anointest my head with oil; my cup runneth over
"(Psalm 23:2-5 KJV).

In a nutshell, proverbs 4:23, NIV says *"Above all else, guard your heart, for everything you do flows from it"*. If you want God to keep you in peace constantly, and use the open dimension to solve all your problems, then practice these things.

Unveiling The Purpose Of The Open Dimension of Tongues

The open dimension of tongues can be experienced during prayer in form of a known tongue or an unknown tongue. It can also be experienced during conversations with people. People have said things they never knew would come to pass carelessly like that. Just because they opened their mouths and a spirit filled it with something. This is why the scripture warned us of filthy jokes: *"Nor should there be obscenity, foolish talk or coarse joking, which are out of place, but rather thanksgiving" (Ephesians 5: 4 KJV)*. People who have no special qualifications and reputations operated in the open dimension of tongues where they had their tongues filled by God Himself. Others also who have relationships with God have also operated in this dimension. See the highlight of the purposes below:

I.   Accurate counsel and advice

The Holy Spirit uses the open dimension of tongues to bring rare and pertinent counsel to people. The scripture says:

"Where no counsel is, the people fall: but in the multitude of counselors, there is safety" (proverbs 11:14).

Below are examples of accurate counsel and advice purposes of the open dimension of tongues:

a.   *The Little maid's advice*

The little maid never heard anything from the Lord, she just spoke and what she said was the solution needed by the commander for His healing and deliverance.

"And the Syrians had gone out by companies, and had brought away captive out of the land of Israel a little maid, and she waited on Naaman's wife.

And she said unto her mistress, Would God my lord were with the prophet that is in Samaria! for he would recover him of his leprosy.

And one went in, and told his lord, saying, Thus and thus said the maid that is of the land of Israel. And the king of Syria said, Go to, go, and I will send a letter unto the king of Israel. And he departed, and took with him ten talents of silver, and six thousand pieces of gold, and ten changes of raiment" (2 Kings 5:2-5 KJV).

b.   Ahithophel's counsel

"And the counsel of Ahithophel, which he counseled in those days, was as if a man had enquired at the oracle of God: so was all the counsel of Ahithophel both with David and with Absalom" (2 Samuel 16:23 KJV).

c.   Advice from Jethro "Moses' father-in-law"

Jethro gave a piece of advice to Moses, at the end of the advice he said "If thou shall do this and God command you so". This tells you Jethro is a lover of God. He fears God and has a form of relationship with Him. Again, another lesson to learn from Jethro is the fact that he also gave Moses an assignment to do. He told him to confirm the matter from the Lord if it will be pleasing to Him. This teaches one never to accept every good-looking piece of advice from people without confirming the piece from God. Don't be fooled to think everyone operates in the open dimension of tongues where the spirit of God fills their tongues. In some cases, it is demons that influence their tongues in careless moments.

"When they have a matter, they come unto me; and I judge between one and another, and I do make them know the statutes of God, and his laws. And Moses' father-in-law said unto him, The thing that thou doest is not good. Thou wilt surely wear away, both thou, and this people that is with thee: for this thing is too heavy for thee; thou art not able to perform it thyself alone. Hearken now unto my voice, I will give thee counsel, and God shall be with thee: Be thou for the people to God-ward, that thou mayest bring the causes unto God: And thou shalt teach them ordinances and laws, and shalt shew them the way wherein they must walk, and the work that they must do. Moreover, thou shalt provide out of all the people able men, such as fear God, men of truth, hating covetousness; and place such over them, to be rulers of thousands, and rulers of hundreds, rulers of fifties, and rulers of tens: And let them judge the people at all seasons: and it shall be, that every great matter they shall bring unto thee, but every small matter they shall judge: so shall it be easier for thyself, and they shall bear the burden with thee. If thou shalt do this thing, and God command thee so, then thou shalt be able to endure, and all these people shall also go to their place in peace" (Exodus 18:16-23 KJV).

ii.   *Praying the right way*

Many times, we go to the place of prayer with our hearts filled with prayer points. Suddenly, we find ourselves praying for the things we never wanted to pray for. We begin to experience an upsurge of words different from the itemized ones in our hearts. Attempts to change it always prove abortive. It is like a burden in the heart. The Spirit is the one who utters those words beyond your self-interest.

"...For it is not ye that speak, but the Spirit of your Father which speaketh in you"
(Mathew 10:20 KJV).

iii.   Victory and acquittal

Jesus argued with the tempter and won the argument. Scriptures popped up in His heart like a well of water. He defeated the tempter (Mathew 4:1-9). Paul the Apostle experienced the same thing while He spoke before King Agrippa (Acts 26:19). The Holy Spirit can speak through believers in this manner in an interview, in a court of law, in debates, or in any gathering where responses are required. This is why the Bible says:

"But when they deliver you up, take no thought how or what ye shall speak: for it shall be given you in that same hour what ye shall speak. For it is not ye that speak, but the Spirit of your Father which speaketh in you" (Mathew 10:19-20 KJV).

The disciples of Jesus walked so much in this realm of the spirit's operation. They spoke words that gave them acquittance before many judges and ill-meaning people. They gave apple pie answers to different questions. Their utterances demystified enigmatic issues. This happened as proof of the Spirit speaking through them.

iv.   Direction

Jethro and Ahithophel were men who operated in this depth. The disciples of Jesus also experienced such a dimension again and again. They spoke words that were infallible in the face of diverse crossroads, oppositions, challenges, and troubles (Acts 2, 4; 6:4, & Acts 15). At many crossroads in the journey of the disciples, the spirit gave certain utterances of direction through many of the apostles. The Apostles never lacked directions. The Holy Ghost spoke to them through the open dimension of tongues in seasons and out of seasons.

v.   Freedom

The intention of God to deliver men from error and freedom is always being made known true this. It is the way of the spirit in setting men free.

"If the Son, therefore, shall make you free, ye shall be free indeed" (John 8: 36 KJV).

The Two Kinds of Open Dimension of Tongues

The known tongue and the unknown tongues are the two kinds of the open dimension of tongues.

Let us begin by analyzing them one after the other:

1.   The Open Dimension of the Known Tongue

The known tongue is for the understanding heart, the fruitful mind expression with the power of the earthly tongue writing, earthly languages, and other earthly native tongues of expressions.

> *"But when they deliver you up, take no thought how or what ye shall speak: for it shall be given you in that same hour what ye shall speak. For it is not ye that speak, but the Spirit of your Father which speaketh in you" (Mathew 10:19-20 KJV).*

Ordinary words can be used as guage for directing and guiding people at the face of oppositions. People can speak words that are impeccable when the spirit fills their tongues, that is, open your mouth and I will fill it.

2.   The Open dimension of the unknown tongue

The unknown tongue is from the Holy Spirit and in conjunction with the human spirit. It's an impact of the Holy Spirit on the human spirit. It enforces divine language on the spirit of man and his tongue to communicate with God and spirit.

> *"For if I pray in an unknown tongue, <u>my spirit prayeth</u>, but my understanding is unfruitful" (1 Corinthians 14:14 KJV).*

The Three Kinds of Forces Acting in the Open Dimension of Tongues

There are three forces that usually hijack this dimension. The force of man, demon, and the Holy Spirit.

1.   The force of man in the open dimension of tongues

This is the situation where it is the man that fills the tongue of another man with what to say. It can be for good; education to win an argument and it can also be for bad. Countless times, people force words into people's mouths. They make them say what they don't want to say. The victims of this usually open their mouths to declare what they were told to say. This is what usually results in false witnesses and false allegations:

"Now the chief priests, and elders, and all the council, sought false witness against Jesus, to put him to death; But found none: yea, though many false witnesses came, yet found they none. At the last came two false witnesses, And said, This fellow said, I am able to destroy the temple of God, and to build it in three days. And the high priest arose, and said unto him, Answerest thou nothing? what is it which these witness against thee? But Jesus held his peace, And the high priest answered and said unto him, I adjure thee by the living God, that thou tell us whether thou be the Christ, the Son of God" (Mathew 26: 59-63 KJV).

2.   The force of demons in the open dimension of tongues

This is usually the case in which demons fill the tongues of people with negative words whenever they open their tongues to talk. It is an irresistible force that makes people curse, abuse and confess negatively without control. The people involved do not usually have control over their tongues. They literally talk like fools and possessed people.

"The tongue of the wise useth knowledge aright: but the mouth of fools poureth out foolishness" (Proverbs 15:2 KJV).

In the fool's category, it is usually for the destruction of himself: *"A fool's lips enter into contention, and his mouth calleth for strokes. A fool's mouth is his destruction, and his lips are the snare of his soul" (Proverbs 18:6-7 KJV).*

Possessed people are the second category of people. Demons make irresistible confessions through their mouths. They are not even aware. If you have ever seen people confessing under the atmosphere of the fire of God, you'll see that they don't even know what they are saying.

"And cried with a loud voice, and said, What have I to do with thee, Jesus, thou Son of the most high God? I adjure thee by God, that thou torment me not. For he said unto him, Come out of the man, thou unclean spirit. And he asked him, What is thy name? And he answered, saying, My name is Legion: for we are many. And he besought him much that he would not send them away out of the country" (Mark 5:7-10 KJV).

In the above scripture, the man's original state was changed to Legion's by the demons living inside him, jettisoning the man's real name without his consent. There are other people who regularly do not guide their words. They open their mouths anyhow and demons fill them up.

These people need the deliverance of their mouths and hearts from the invasion of demons. The third category is careless people. They are usually ebbing and flowing when it comes to speaking ill words. This is not because they are foolish but because they are sometimes carried away by jokes or the pain of what they are feeling. Owing to this rippling behavior, they confess negatively. They give-in to the pressure of life and the situations surrounding them. Hence, they are subdued by life.

> *"But I tell you that everyone will have to give account on the day of judgment for every empty word they have spoken. For by your words, you will be acquitted, and by your words you will be condemned." (Mathew 12:36-37 NIV).*

> *"Nor should there be obscenity, foolish talk or coarse joking, which are out of place, but rather thanksgiving." (Ephesians 5:4 NIV).*

3.   The force of the Holy Spirit in the open Dimension of tongues

The Holy Spirit does speak words. He does these things many times in many ways. He puts words in one's mouths without one being conscious in any way. The saints of God, preachers and every one can literally speak words that are orchestrated by the Holy Spirit and not know that it is the Holy Spirit influencing them.

> *"For it is not ye that speak, but the Spirit of your Father which speaketh in you"*
> *(Mathew 10:19-20 KJV).*

What one needs to operate this dimension is the yielded life to the Holy Spirit. The more yielded you are, the more the Holy Spirit speaks through you.

Operating In the Open Dimension of Tongues In the Place of Prayer

A few years of experience from many matured people who have operated in this realm would be a great example to explore. Someone once said, "Each time I pray in an unknown tongue, I usually operate in the open dimension of tongues. I don't premeditate my words and the codes of the unknown tongues. I don't come with a stolen type of tongue either. Rather, when I appear before the Lord, I do so with an open heart and He fills my tongue with His spirit.

How can one achieve this? It works like your mouth is moving in the place of prayers but your heart is not functioning for any meditation. This is the way the Lord touches the mouths;

> *"Then the Lord put forth his hand, and touched my mouth. And the Lord said unto me, Behold, I have put my words in thy mouth" (Jeremiah 1:9 KJV).*

This is not by just opening your mouth into the air and expecting someone to just be filling it with air. No! It is a form of speaking that leaves the heart without clues. No understanding of the heart. Sometimes, the words can also be heard with the ears. In some cases, some people's mouths move faster than anything you can ever imagine.

Most believers, at the beginning of their Christian journeys, when they received the baptism of the spirit with the evidence of speaking in tongues, of course, a reaction took place in their hearts first but the rest of the work was in their mouths and tongues. Their mouths moved with so much energy that after the experience they thought they could no longer speak in tongues. Someone said he slapped himself, trying to control his mouth but could not. The mouth was moving but the heart could not stop the mouth from saying something. The heart thought to stop but the mouth would not. I have had people who complained so much to me that their mouths could not be controlled due to the influence of the spirit on their mouths during their first speaking-in-tongues experience. They kept talking nonstop. The Spirit had touched their tongue with an irresistible influence.

A few nuggets will be highlighted below for an easy understanding of how to operate in this dimension in the place of prayer:

1. Understanding the infilling of the heart and the mouth with words beyond artifice and great intentions:
    "Then the Lord put forth his hand, and touched my mouth. And the Lord said unto me, Behold, I have put my words in thy mouth" (Jeremiah 1:9 KJV).

2. Understanding the divine tug to open your mouth wide in trust:
    "I am the Lord thy God, which brought thee out of the land of Egypt: open thy mouth wide, and I will fill it" (Psalm 81:10 KJV).
    "And I have put my words in thy mouth, and I have covered thee in the shadow of mine hand, that I may plant the heavens, and lay the foundations of the earth, and say unto Zion, Thou art my people" (Isaiah 51:16 KJV).

3. Understanding an open divine portal's impact on the mouth:
   One can come in contact with divine portals that can make one speak words. Angels' activity within a region or a location can provoke an immediate impact on the mouth to say and confess the divinity of God without apology.
   "And Jacob awaked out of his sleep, and he said, Surely the Lord is in this place; and I knew it not" (Genesis 28:16 KJV).

4. Flexibility with the Holy Spirit "the trust-wheel":
   "Trust in the Lord with all thine heart; and lean not unto thine own understanding. In all thy ways acknowledge him, and he shall direct thy paths. Be not wise in thine own eyes: fear the Lord, and depart from evil" (Proverbs 3:6-7 KJV).

5. Faith in the instruction of the Holy Spirit:
   "For as many as are led by the Spirit of God, they are the sons of God" (Romans 8:14 KJV).

6. Obedience to the voice of the spirit:
   "If ye be willing and obedient, ye shall eat the good of the land" (Isaiah 1:19 KJV).

The knowledge of the eruption of the mouth with divine will is important in the place of prayers. It helps you know that something urgent can keep distracting your tongue. It can seem like the sleep of the tongue but not so usually. This is the tug in the tongue. It is proof that one can trust God enough to pray whatever God puts in his mouth.

> *"For if I pray in an unknown tongue, my spirit prayeth, but my understanding is unfruitful. What is it then? I will pray with the spirit, and I will pray with the understanding also: I will sing with the spirit, and I will sing with the understanding also" (1 Corinthians 14:14-15 KJV).*

Again, this experience can be an experience for both the known and the unknown tongues in the place of prayers. A fruitful understanding can operate in such a way that one can abandon his personal intentions in the place of prayers and begin to pray for certain name(s) that keep interrupting one's tongues. This is a sign that the Lord is in the place of prayer.

Key Activation Prayers

Awesome Holy Spirit come upon me with your fresh power and anointing with the audacity to operate in the open dimension of tongues whether in a known or an unknown tongue. Release the burning fire upon me. Activate this dimension right now in Jesus' name. Amen!

Chapter

10

THE HEARING DIMENSION OF TONGUES

CHAPTER TEN

THE HEARING DIMENSION OF TONGUES

"And thine ears shall hear a word behind thee, saying, this is the way, walk ye in it,
when ye turn to the right hand, and when ye turn to the left"
(Isaiah 30:21 KJV)

The hearing dimension combines the open dimension with the audible voice for full operation. Every voice is a tongue, because it communicates messages. Hearing the voice of God is the same as hearing the tongues of Elohim. The diversity of God's mode of communication is what gives birth to countless number of tongues existing in both spiritual and physical horizons. God's system of communication is so advanced that it takes care of the communication of angels and that of all humans. The hearing dimension of the tongue is a state where the entity called "the voice" brings the whole essence and existence of the spirit, angels, or a person to you. Nevertheless, we will be talking about the Holy Spirit and His angels. If you observe the scripture above, you would see that the Bible says "You would hear a voice from behind". It is the utmost desire of God that we hear His voice. Success in any area of life can be tremendous and seamless when our choices are preceded by the accurate voice of God for effective directions. All prayers are reflections of desires. This is the reason God never wants us to go astray following wrong desires. He gave us the Holy Ghost so that after the departure of Christ, we can still be led by his counterpart. He wants to make His intentions known to us in many ways so that our steps and our choices are guided accurately.

Going forward, we will understand the hearing dimension of the tongue by following the theme scripture above. No one who is born again and identified with the person of Christ can be anything in life without the voice of God. This is why the scripture says *"And thine ears shall hear a word behind thee, saying, This is the way, walk ye in it, when ye turn to the right hand, and when ye turn to the left" (Isaiah 30:21 KJV).* Did you observe it says your ears? Did you also observe it says "shall hear a word from behind"? The scripture never said from within in this case. It is also important to know that it is the voice that conveys words. We have three kinds of voices:

i.   Celestial voices within- the Holy Spirit or the Godhead.

ii.   External Celestial voices- The voice of the Spirit upon, Angels and demons.

iii.   The Terrestrial voices of men.

    There are two ways celestial voices can be transmitted to man:

i.   Celestial Voice Transmitting from Within.

ii.   Celestial Voices Transmitting From External Environment (Behind, Beside, In Front, above, and so on).

The Celestial Voice Transmitting from Within

There are two kinds of celestial voices transmitting from within. The first one is the synchronized long-time impression of the word and the spirit regularly influencing the mind; it is called "conscience. Another name for this is the witness in the Holy Ghost or witness together with the Holy Ghost as some translations of the Bible call it. *"I say the truth in Christ, I lie not, my conscience also bearing me witness in the Holy Ghost" (Romans 9:1 KJV).*

The second celestial voice transmitting from within is the direct voice of the Holy Spirit influencing the conscience of the mind. *"As they ministered to the Lord, and fasted, the Holy Ghost said, Separate me Barnabas and Saul for the work whereunto I have called them" (Acts 13:2 KJV).* Also, if the spirit within a man is unrenewed, such persons are susceptible to hearing the voice of demons. In the same vein, the voice within can bring the voice of demons to possessed people. Look at what the scripture says:

"Create in me a clean heart, O God; and renew a right spirit within me" (Psalm 51:10 KJV). This tells you that the renewed and transfigured spirit of the believer is within him. Notwithstanding, an unrenewed spirit either demonic or natural can be within an unbeliever. Furthermore, the scripture says *"Hereby know we that we dwell in him, and he in us, because he hath given us of his Spirit" (1 John4:13 KJV).* The spirit that Jesus has given us breaks the code of the voice of God within.

The Holy Spirit reveals God and the things of the Spirit to us from within. He gives us God's instructions directly from within. *"Know ye not that ye are the temple of God, and that the Spirit of God dwelleth in you?" (1 Corinthians 3:16 KJV).* There is a depth of instruction that comes from the Holy Spirit whom we have received. He teaches and guides us always from within.

"But you have received the Holy Spirit, and he lives within you, so you don't need anyone to teach you what is true. For the Spirit teaches you everything you need to know, and what he teaches is true—it is not a lie. So just as he has taught you, remain in fellowship with Christ" (1 John 2:27 NLT).

All followers of Christ are like a flock of sheep. A sheep follows the voice of the shepherd not necessarily anyone that looks like Him but the voice. Whenever the sheep hear the voice of the shepherd, they move toward the direction of the voice. God uses the voice dimension to lead us in life and in the place of prayer. This is why the Bible says *"My sheep hear my voice, and I know them, and they follow me" (John 10:27 KJV).*

The Celestial Voices Transmitting from External Environment

The voice of God can come to a man from an external environment. In this way, He can make Himself known to that man. Mathew 3:17 says *"And lo a voice from heaven, saying, this is my beloved Son, in whom I am well pleased"*. This is what I call the order of the spirit upon the chosen ones. It is the portrayal of the spirit's manifestation as the almighty from the external source.

Now, I will explain the manifestations of God as a celestial voice transmitting from the earth realm and I will also do justice to the other celestial voices transmitting information in the earth realm as well.

i.   God's voice without visible body:

This is when the voice of God comes to a man without any visible body. God echoes His name before an earthly body as Almighty. He delivers His message through this means. You would not see the body but you would hear His audible voice: *"And lo a voice from heaven, saying, this is my beloved Son, in whom I am well pleased"* (Mathew 3: 17). This reality usually comes with voice alone.

ii.   God's voice with visible body:

This can be the theophanic manifestation of God in earthly realms or the manifestation of the Spirit of God with a celestial body. This visibility is in two ways. He can use the celestial but human-like body, and He can also use the spiritual but visible body in His appearance. For instance, Melchizedek appeared in the flesh of man but was a celestial being:

"And Melchizedek king of Salem brought forth bread and wine: and he was the priest of the most high God. And he blessed him, and said, Blessed be Abram of the most high God, possessor of heaven and earth" (Genesis 14:18-19).

God appeared and spoke in a spiritual but visible form to Moses:
"And the angel of the Lord appeared unto him in a flame of fire out of the midst of a bush: and he looked, and, behold, the bush burned with fire, and the bush was not consumed. And Moses said, I will now turn aside, and see this great sight, why the bush is not burnt. And when the Lord saw that he turned aside to see, God called unto him out of the midst of the bush, and said, Moses, Moses. And he said, Here am I. And he said, Draw not nigh hither: put off thy shoes from off thy feet, for the place whereon thou standest is holy ground" (Exodus 3:2-5 KJV).

God appeared and spoke to Abraham in a bodily form. He even ate food in Abraham's house. Abraham took care of Him and the angels that accompanied Him:

"And the Lord appeared unto him in the plains of Mamre: and he sat in the tent door in the heat of the day; And the Lord said, Shall I hide from Abraham that thing which I do; Seeing that Abraham shall surely become a great and mighty nation, and all the nations of the earth shall be blessed in him?" (Genesis 18:1, 17-18 KJV):

iii.   The voice of God's angels with visible bodies:
The voice of God's angels can come to us with the visible manifestation of the body of the angels. The manifestations can be in both the human-like body form and the spiritual body form. In rare cases, one can receive the tongue of angels and host the body at the same time, but in most cases, people only host the tongues of angels in visions or in prayers. Let us examine the two forms listed above;

1.   The voice of God's angels in the visible human-like body form: This is usually an appearance like that of a man. They can be physically touched in some cases. They can even eat food. They can pass the night in a house. They usually have enough time to carry out the agenda of God on earth when operating in this dimension. Joshua hosted both the voice and the body of these angels. *"As Joshua was sizing up the city of Jericho, a man appeared nearby with a drawn sword. Joshua strode over to him and demanded, "Are you friend or foe?" "I am the Commander-in-Chief of the Lord's army," he replied. Joshua fell to the*

ground before him and worshiped him and said, "Give me your commands."(Joshua 5:13-14 TLB).

Abraham also hosted the accompanying angels of God both in their bodies and voices. *"The Lord appeared again to Abraham while he was living in the oak grove at Mamre. This is the way it happened: One hot summer afternoon as he was sitting in the opening of his tent, he suddenly noticed three men coming toward him. He sprang up and ran to meet them and welcomed them. "Sirs," he said, "please don't go any farther. Stop awhile and rest here in the shade of this tree while I get water to refresh your feet, and a bite to eat to strengthen you. Do stay awhile before continuing your journey." "All right," they said, "do as you have said." (Genesis 18:1-4 TLB).*

Lot hosted the angels' tongues and bodies. They ate food and slept over at his house. *"That evening the two angels came to the entrance of the city of Sodom, and Lot was sitting there as they arrived. When he saw them he stood up to meet them, and welcomed them. "Sirs," he said, "come to my home as my guests for the night; you can get up as early as you like and be on your way again." "Oh, no thanks," they said, "we'll just stretch out here along the street." But he was very urgent, until at last they went home with him, and he set a great feast before them, complete with freshly baked unleavened bread. After the meal" Genesis 19:1-3 KJV).*

2.   The voice of God's angels in visible spiritual bodies:
In this situation, angels appear with their spiritual bodies. They usually can appear with some protective glory around them. At other times, they can also appear without any protective glory round about them but still maintain their spiritual body. These scriptural examples are manifestations of such;
"Suddenly an angel appeared among them, and the landscape shone bright with the glory of the Lord. They were badly frightened, but the angel reassured them. "Don't be afraid!" he said. "I bring you the most joyful news ever announced, and it is for everyone! The Savior—yes, the Messiah, the Lord—has been born tonight in Bethlehem! How will you recognize him? You will find a baby wrapped in a blanket, lying in a manger!"
Suddenly, the angel was joined by a vast host of others—the armies of heaven—praising God:
"Glory to God in the highest heaven," they sang, "and peace on earth for all those pleasing him." (Luke 2:9-14 TLB).

These angels are seen in visions in their spiritual bodies. They can be seen physically, and at some other times with spiritual eyes. The difference between the spiritual body and the human form is the state. In this state, they don't usually eat food, drink water or pass the night in a house. They have limited time to return to base. Like in the case of Jacob's encounter with the angel of God, "the angel pleaded with Jacob to let Him go because the day breaks" (Gen 32: 25-26). They always like to deliver the purpose on target without wasting much time. There are times they can be discerned with the inner eyes or seen physically. They can also be seen while sleeping or when one is awake, or be seen while one is praying. Let's see the following examples;

• Cornelius' wide-awake vision of angels
"While wide awake one afternoon he had a vision—it was about three o'clock—and in this vision, he saw an angel of God coming toward him. "Cornelius!" the angel said.

Cornelius stared at him in terror. "What do you want, sir?" he asked the angel. And the angel replied, "Your prayers and charities have not gone unnoticed by God!" (Acts 10:3-4 TLB).

The difference between the spiritual body and the human form is the state.

• Zechariah's prayer time vision of angels
Zechariah was in the place of prayers when He received the tongue of an angel. The angel came to him in a spiritual body. In this state, they don't usually relate much to earthly things like eating and others.

"Meanwhile, a great crowd stood outside in the Temple court, praying as they always did during that part of the service when the incense was being burned. Zacharias was in the sanctuary when suddenly an angel appeared, standing to the right of the altar of incense! Zacharias was startled and terrified. But the angel said, "Don't be afraid, Zacharias! For I have come to tell you that God has heard your prayer, and your wife, Elizabeth, will bear you a son! And you are to name him John. You will both have great joy and gladness at his birth, and many will rejoice with you" (Luke 1:10-14 TLB).

• Mary's wide-awake vision of Angels
In the encounter of Mary in her wide-awake state, she saw the angel in his spiritual body. No additional relationship was demanded by the angel, no eating, and no drinking!

"The following month God sent the angel Gabriel to Nazareth, a village in Galilee, to a virgin, Mary, engaged to be married to a man named Joseph, a descendant of King David. Gabriel appeared to her and said, "Congratulations, favored lady! The Lord is with you!" Confused and disturbed, Mary tried to think what the angel could mean.

"Don't be frightened, Mary," the angel told her, "for God has decided to wonderfully bless you! Very soon now, you will become pregnant and have a baby boy, and you are to name him 'Jesus.' He shall be very great and shall be called the Son of God. And the Lord God shall give him the throne of his ancestor David. And he shall reign over Israel forever; his Kingdom shall never end!"

Mary asked the angel, "But how can I have a baby? I am a virgin."The angel replied, "The Holy Spirit shall come upon you, and the power of God shall overshadow you; so the baby born to you will be utterly holy—the Son of God. Furthermore, six months ago your Aunt Elizabeth—'the barren one,' they called her—became pregnant in her old age!" (Luke 1:26-37 TLB).

iv.   The voice of God's angels only

There are times when one can hear the tongue of angels without seeing any vision. The voice can just come to you without any bodily expression form. This is common with many believers. They operate in the hearing dimension of tongues. They receive the accurate voice of God's angels in their places of work and in their day-to-day activities without deception. If it is the voice of God's holy angels, it usually does not come with deception but direction in the will of God.

"And thine ears shall hear a word behind thee, saying, this is the way, walk ye in it, when ye turn to the right hand, and when ye turn to the left" (Isaiah 30:21 KJV).

v.   The voice of fallen angels with visible bodies

Demons are the spirits of the fallen angels. They use deceptions. They push deception into the minds of people. They keep on lying to people. They are the likes of the voice of familiar spirits deceiving people to go against the will of God. Be careful with them, they can come in the face of humans, forms, shapes, and symbols.

*"And no marvel; for Satan himself is transformed into an angel of light" (2 Corinthians 11:14 KJV).*The manifestation of spirits generally includes physical and spiritual body forms, shapes, and symbols. This is why the Scripture says *"Then a spirit passed before my*

face; the hair of my flesh stood up: It stood still, but I could not discern the form thereof: an image was before mine eyes, there was silence, and I heard a voice, saying" (Job 4:15-16 KJV). Test all the spirits!

vi.   The voice of demons without any visible body

This has to do with hearing voices and seeing nobody. Subject every angelic voice to the accurate will of God. If it negates the will of God, quickly discern that it is of the devil.

The Key Thing to do in The Hearing Dimension

Obedience to God in the hearing dimension of the tongue is very important. Hear the tongue and obey. Disobedience jeopardizes instructions.

"Whether it be good, or whether it be evil, we will obey the voice of the Lord our God, to whom we send thee; that it may be well with us, when we obey the voice of the Lord our God" (Jeremiah 42:6 KJV).

Hearing the voice of God is not tantamount to obedience. *"While it is said, today if ye will hear his voice, harden not your hearts, as in the provocation" (Hebrew 3:15 KJV).*

"Switching Speaking in Tongues to The Hearing Dimension"

This is judging in prayers as you hear. Jesus had the spirit without measure. He operated in the hearing dimension as much as He operated in the dimension of the spirit within.

"I can of mine own self do nothing: as I hear, I judge: and my judgment is just; because I seek not mine own will, but the will of the Father which hath sent me" (John 5:30 KJV).

This is usually for people who are mature in their walk with God. You can switch tongues to the hearing dimension. Whether to judge life matters or make decisions. In this case, you'll begin to operate with the angel of interpretation, will, and purpose. The angel of His presence can stand with you and begin to bring you words and interpretation in your ears. It is like picking your intended words from the guardian angels that are standing by your side to put words in your mouth. This is more than just the "open and fill it" dimension of tongues. It is in recognition of the person standing and talking with you, the one you are hearing. It is being conscious of the person who wants to constantly touch your ears as much as He does to the tongues.

"Then the Lord put forth his hand, and touched my mouth. And the Lord said unto me, Behold, I have put my words in thy mouth" (Jeremiah 1:9 KJV).

"I am the Lord thy God, which brought thee out of the land of Egypt: open thy mouth wide, and I will fill it" (Psalm 81:10 KJV).

Long time ago, I met someone who had a dream where he was surrounded by a host of enemies, and someone told him to be saying a certain word like "glasio banito legwa" a tongue he was never familiar with the meaning. By saying this, all the enemies died in the dream due to the overpowering potency of those words.

The same thing does happen in real life. It has happened to me on several occasions. There were moments and days when I wanted to pray and the guardian angel would begin to tell me this is what you should say in tongues. I usually feel energized when I pray like this. I know there would be no room for recycling anybody's tongue but it would be time to pray in the spirit's will and directly from the throne of God.

Operating In the Hearing Dimension of Tongues at The Place of Prayers

Over the years, I have had experiences, where I was praying and suddenly began hearing a man's voice at the same time saying things to my ears. I did not see anyone. I never knew what to pray for initially. Suddenly, the voice started talking to my ears. The man began to tell me names, I started calling the names and praying for the people. He spoke tongues to my ears, and I was speaking the tongues too. Later on, after the prayer, I realized I had prayed for people who were just on their way coming to see me for counseling and prayers. I spoke the mysteries which he spoke to my ears. I uttered the solutions to their problems in the place of prayers without knowing that these people were even on their way coming to meet me for the first time. Initially, my purpose of starting the prayer was to pray for myself, but God interrupted it.

"And thine ears shall hear a word behind thee, saying, this is the way, walk ye in it, when ye turn to the right hand, and when ye turn to the left" (Isaiah 30:21 KJV).

Someone may ask, what do I do in the place of prayer? How do I connect? First of all, you need to know that, the decision of what is revealed to you and what can be revealed to you is usually up to God. Our responsibility is to prepare and make every part of us ready to receive from Him in the place of prayers. Make yourself yielded every time you come to the place of prayers. Is it not amazing to know that the specific word, names, and tongues that I needed to speak were given to me in the place of prayer? I was hearing them with my ears and not my heart. It is possible for God to give the same information to people like that in their hearts while praying. It is possible to even hear those names in your heart. One thing you just need to know is that there is a difference between hearing it in your heart and hearing it in your ears. The ears' experience is different from the hearts'.

The experience is like, when another man is talking to your ears. It is like when you are paying attention to hearing the full gist of a matter in your ears from your friend. Have you ever been praying and it's like people are opening the doors in your house and you had to quickly go check and you see no one? Have you ever been praying and it is like someone is knocking on your door? Have you ever been praying and it is like people are marching in? If the answer is yes, then you are in the hearing dimension of tongues. You only need to grow up so that you can operate better with a higher level of understanding. Below is a list of the few things you can do to walk in this dimension:

1. Be conscious of the guardian angel who may want to touch your tongue.
2. Always pay attention in the place of prayer.
3. Attend to whatever the Lord may bring to your hearing in the place of prayer.
4. Uphold the faith and do away with fear.
5. Seek understanding because understanding gives value to hearing.
6. You might have to ask God questions when you have the hearing encounter.
7. You might need a depth of wisdom and revelation gift to connect the dots especially when the names of people are called.
8. Learn to switch tongues to the hearing dimension.
9. Connect yourself to the frequency of the guardian angel who stands to put words in your mouth.
10. You might have to increase your prayer fire, energy, and time in the place of prayers.

Key Activation Prayers

Father in the name of Jesus, release the grace for the activation of this dimension. Let your Holy Spirit open my ears to begin to hear divine tongues as the Lord will

Chapter

11

THE 2-DIMENSIONAL
GROANING OF TONGUES

CHAPTER ELEVEN
THE 2-DIMENSIONAL GROANING OF TONGUES

"Likewise, the Spirit also helpeth our infirmities: for we know not what we should pray for as we ought: but the Spirit itself maketh intercession for us with groanings which cannot be uttered" (Romans 8:26 KJV).

Groanings are Spirit's utterances that are wordless. They are deep moans of the spirit's grief and pain. They are indicative of spiritual annoyance and insistence. They are harsh sounds of deep request in the spirit under a prolonged strain. They cannot be expressed in words but with deep sighs and great force. They are insistent requests placed with deep moans due to imminent trouble and needs.

The realm of spiritual groaning is two (2) dimensional. This dimension includes man, and God's creation. As we continue, we will look into this. Looking at Jesus' behavior according to the definition earlier. You would see the great concern that He showed towards Lazarus:

"Jesus, therefore, when he saw her weeping, and the Jews who came with her weeping, did groan in the spirit and troubled himself, and he said, Where have ye laid him?' they say to him, `Sir, come and see" (John 11:33 KJV).

Jesus groaned in the spirit and troubled Himself means "He offered a deep prayer to God for His friend". He presented the most valid reasons Lazarus should not die. He did that in the Spirit. His repeated groanings were enough signs of His desire for Lazarus to live on earth. Even though people were there, Jesus took all to Himself a sustained atmosphere of groaning in the Spirit. Jesus wept in addition to the groaning (John 11:35, KJV). Most groanings come with weeping when praying although not at all times. People who groan in the place of prayer usually demonstrate the compassion that convinces God of why He needs to grant their requests while they are praying. The groaning captures their spirits. It renders it broken and tender before the Lord. Again, let's see what more happened to Jesus:

"Jesus therefore again groaning in himself cometh to the grave. It was a cave, and a stone lay upon it. Jesus said, Take ye away the stone. Martha, the sister of him that was

dead, saith unto him, Lord, by this time he stinketh: for he hath been dead four days. Jesus saith unto her, Said I not unto thee, that if thou wouldest believe, thou shouldest see the glory of God?" (John 11:38-40 KJV).

Groanings are deep utterances for making requests known to God. It is the Spirit's way of causing things to happen in nature. The spiritual way of changing an impossibility and turning them into possibility. Groaning tongues are usually heartfelt and soul apprehensive. It's one thing that does not leave a vacuum for unbelief in a praying person. It always swallows all forms of weaknesses.

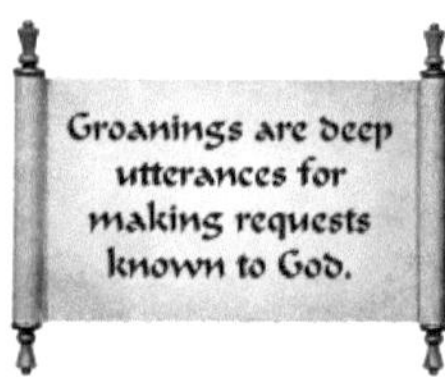

Groanings in the Spirit are God's recipe for overthrowing spiritual weaknesses: "And the Holy Spirit helps us in our weakness. For example, we don't know what God wants us to pray for. But the Holy Spirit prays for us with groanings that cannot be expressed in words" (Romans 8:26 NLT).

Our daily problems are well presented through groaning by the Holy Spirit:

"And in the same way—by our faith—the Holy Spirit helps us with our daily problems and in our praying. For we don't even know what we should pray for nor how to pray as we should, but the Holy Spirit prays for us with such feeling that it cannot be expressed in words" (Romans 8:26 TLB).

Every believer should allow the Holy Spirit to groan in them when He senses the need. Don't quench the spirit. Whenever there is an urge for groaning in your spirit during prayer, please allow it. Push it out!

Polishing off the experience of Jesus, you and I know that Jesus is Lord, and He is God Himself. If God almighty would demonstrate such a thing, a high level of compassion leading to intercession, then this pre-informs you about what the spirit of anyone that receives Him will truly do per time. You and I cannot be exempted from acting the same way when He is touched by our life's circumstances and our infirmities. However, the scripture says;

"For we have not an high priest which cannot be touched with the feeling of our infirmities; but was in all points tempted like as we are, yet without sin" (Hebrews 4:15 KJV).

Jesus is our high priest.

There are two (2) dimensions of groanings. Spiritual man's dimension of groaning and creation dimension of groaning. These two are very essential to our further study.

The Spiritual Man's Dimension of Groaning

Groaning in tongue is a spiritual phenomenon in Christ. It is not within the scope of a natural man's wisdom. A natural man will call it a mere groaning but a spiritual man will call it a dimension of prayer, a deep utterance. Only those who have received the Spirit of God are permitted to operate in this dimension. These are no other people than the spiritually minded people.

> *"Now we have received, not the spirit of the world, but the spirit which is of God; that we might know the things that are freely given to us of God. Which things also we speak, not in the words which man's wisdom teacheth, but which the Holy Ghost teacheth; comparing spiritual things with spiritual. But the natural man receiveth not the things of the Spirit of God: for they are foolishness unto him: neither can he know them, because they are spiritually discerned" (1 Corinthians 2:12-14 KJV).*

Thanks be to God we are spiritually minded to discern both good and bad. We are now born again. We are the people of God. We can receive the things of God. Hence, we'll look at the spiritual man's dimension of groaning. There are two elements needed for this scrutiny:

1. Spiritually discerned burdens

These are divine prayer encumbrances. They are like divine intercessory weights in our spirits. This experience can take place in two ways:

   i.   The burdens of the Holy Spirit to defeat our personal weaknesses and challenges: The devil usually defies and defeats our faith through unforeseen challenges. Our walk of faith is being accosted with so many issues. Some are little besetting sins, weights of rejections, unyielding challenges, oppositions, and demonic trials. These challenges do pose a lot of weaknesses to our spirits, making us unable to pray.

"Cast thy burden upon the Lord, and he shall sustain thee: he shall never suffer the righteous to be moved" (Psalm 55:22 KJV).
"Come unto me, all ye that labour and are heavy laden, and I will give you rest.
Take my yoke upon you, and learn of me; for I am meek and lowly in heart: and ye shall find rest unto your souls" (Mathew 11:28-30 KJV).

Some other times, we have not sinned or done anything wrong, but have no quality discernment to know that trouble is looming in our direction. Hence, the Holy Spirit helps our weaknesses in prayer. When we open our mouths to pray, He begins to utter words beyond our understanding through groanings to neutralize the projections of the devil that were fired against us.

"Likewise, the Spirit also helpeth our infirmities: for we know not what we should
pray for as we ought: but the Spirit itself maketh intercession for us with groanings which cannot be uttered" (Romans 8:26 KJV).

A good illustration of this is the story of a woman who felt the urge to pray. She groaned again and again not knowing which direction to focus on in her place of prayer. She eventually groaned for about 2 hours. Later at night, armed robbers came to her street and raided all the neighboring houses. They equally injured several people, but the house of this woman was exempted from their demonic operations. She was the only person that was spared. Hallelujah!

ii.   The burdens of the Holy Spirit to intercede and apprehend people's troubles: There are times when the Holy Spirit lays tugging issues in our hearts. We keep receiving these recurring signals and flashes in our spirits. They are usually unavoidable and inescapable loads. The more we try to shy away from them, the more the Holy Spirit keeps flashing them in our hearts. Sometimes, we get stucked in the urge that we do not even know "the how and the what" to pray for. All we can even do in that place of prayer, is to groan and groan again. Words will fade. One's understanding might sometimes be unfruitful. However, the only thing that will keep flowing in those moments is groaning. A good example is the story of a father who felt the urge to groan in the place of prayer. He groaned in prayer for about an hour in his car not knowing exactly why. Just about two hours later, a car hit his child in the school. He got the news that the boy was hit so badly by a derailed vehicle but nothing happened to the child. No bruises and no injuries. This was because the father had prayed earlier.

2.   The Burdens of Instant Faith Confrontations (when Someone Runs to You for Help): Every believer goes through seasons where they are faced with open confrontations against their faith through the need to help others. Sometimes, it may come like a hunch. However, most of the time, it comes vis-à-vis.

"Bear ye one another's burdens, and so fulfill the law of Christ" (Galatians 6:2 KJV).

Lazarus' death is an example of such. Where Jesus was in a face-to-face experience with the death-grave of Lazarus. He was under an obligation to do something. His profession of faith and recent work of wonders were all put to the test. People were expecting an instant solution from Him in the face of this challenge:

"Jesus therefore again groaning in himself cometh to the grave. It was a cave, and a stone lay upon it. Jesus said, Take ye away the stone. Martha, the sister of him that was dead, saith unto him, Lord, by this time he stinketh: for he hath been dead four days. Jesus saith unto her, Said I not unto thee, that if thou wouldest believe, thou shouldest see the glory of God?" (John 11:38-40 KJV).

Just as Jesus did groan severally to solve the problem, periodically the Lord also positions us in places where we can be able to attend to the troubles of people. For instance, someone can call you to come and pray for a person who is feeling unwell. Remember, you may not have many details about the sickness or even know the root cause. The only thing the Holy Spirit may need to do is to bring solutions to light through you.

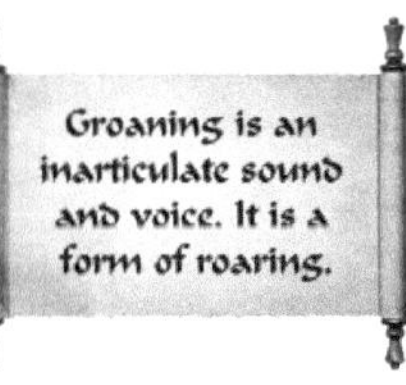

The Creation's Dimension Of Groaning

A groaning is an inarticulate sound and voice. It is a form of roaring. It's an inarticulate voice that can convey many things like pleasure, displeasure, pain, and so on. This dimension of reality is what emphasizes the underlying purpose of the voice and sound in everything that God has created. Although, there may not be expressible utterances but only groaning, yet there is a deep interpretation when the revelation light is turned on.

"For we know that the whole creation groaneth and travaileth in pain together until now. And not only they but ourselves also, which have the firstfruits of the Spirit, even we ourselves groan within ourselves, waiting for the adoption, to wit, the redemption of our body" (Romans 8:22-23 KJV).

The decay that crept into creation is what culminates in the groaning of creation and men. All creation came out from the mouth of God. Jesus is the firstborn of all creatures. All creatures share in His identity. This prepense is what gave creatures the power to act like humans. He's the root of the voice and ability to relate with divinity. All things consist of him.

"Who is the image of the invisible God, the firstborn of every creature: For by him were all things created, that are in heaven, and that are in earth, visible and invisible, whether they be thrones, or dominions, or principalities, or powers: all things were created by him, and for him: And he is before all things, and by him all things consist. And he is the head of the body, the church: who is the beginning, the firstborn from the dead; that in all things he might have the preeminence" (Colossians 1:15-18 KJV).

All Creation Has Sense Organs And The Voice Code Of Breath
There is a code of breath in everything created by God. Therefore, we can say all creation has a voice, eyes, and ears. They all have life. They have the type of life that came out from the word of God and the breath of His mouth. They all can see and can hear. For instance,

I.   The earth has a mouth and ears
"And the earth helped the woman, and the earth opened her mouth, and *swallowed up the flood which the dragon cast out of his mouth (Revelations 12:16 KJV).*
"O earth, earth, earth, hear the word of the Lord" (Jeremiah 22:29KJV).

ii.   Men are like trees
The trees of the field have the potential ability to hear and speak. This is the reason the Bible likened man to trees on many occasions: *"And he shall be like a tree planted by the rivers of water, that bringeth forth his fruit in his season; his leaf also shall not wither; and whatsoever he doeth shall prosper". (Psalms 1:3 KJV).*
When you think about this possibility, then you can think of trees sharing similar

sense organs to men. Righteous men are like trees. The man Jesus prayed for said "I see men like trees, walking" (Mark 8:24).

iii. Jesus also spoke to the fig tree

Can you imagine you talking to a tree? This is weird! Anyone who does this in this age and time will be considered insane, but Jesus did it because men are like trees, and in another realm of life trees are like men: *"And when he saw a fig tree in the way, he came to it, and found nothing thereon, but leaves only, and said unto it, Let no fruit grow on thee henceforward forever. And presently the fig tree withered away" (Mathew 21:19 KJV).*

iv. The trees sought kings

There is an amazing story in the Bible that is a metaphor that adumbrates both spiritual and physical significance as well as the capability of the trees in different realms created by God.

"The trees went forth on a time to anoint a king over them; and they said unto the olive tree, Reign thou over us. But the olive tree said unto them, Should I leave my fatness, wherewith by me they honour God and man, and go to be promoted over the trees? And the trees said to the fig tree, Come thou, and reign over us. But the fig tree said unto them, Should I forsake my sweetness, and my good fruit, and go to be promoted over the trees? Then said the trees unto the vine, Come thou, and reign over us. And the vine said unto them, Should I leave my wine, which cheereth God and man, and go to be promoted over the trees? Then said all the trees unto the bramble, Come thou, and reign over us. And the bramble said unto the trees, If in truth ye anoint me king over you, then come and put your trust in my shadow: and if not, let fire come out of the bramble, and devour the cedars of Lebanon" (Judges 9:8-15 KJV)

v. The mountains and the Hills Break forth into singing

"For ye shall go out with joy, and be led forth with peace: the mountains and the hills shall break forth before you into singing, and all the trees of the field shall clap their hands" (Isaiah 55:12 KJV).

vi. The Ass saw into the Spirit Realms

An Ass is just supposed to see only physical things but, in this case, it saw beyond the physical. There were servants of Balaam that were standing close to the Ass and Balaam. Not one of them could see the angel of the Lord but only the Ass. The Ass saw an angel as much as it saw the people around its master. Imagine a donkey seeing what men cannot see! This is to tell you that every creature has a code of God's breath, and can discern His superior power.

"And Balaam rose up in the morning, and saddled his ass, and went with the princes of Moab. And God's anger was kindled because he went: and the angel of the Lord stood in the way for an adversary against him. Now he was riding upon \ his ass, and his two servants were with him. And the ass saw the angel of the Lord standing in the way, and his sword drawn in his hand: and the ass turned aside out of the way, and went into the field: and Balaam smote the ass, to turn her into the way. But the angel of the Lord stood in a path of the vineyards, a wall being on this side, and a wall on that side. And when the ass saw the angel of the Lord, she thrust herself unto the wall, and crushed Balaam's foot against the wall: and he smote her again. And the angel of the Lord went further, and stood in a narrow place, where was no way to turn either to the right hand or to the left. And when the ass saw the angel of the Lord, she fell down under Balaam: and Balaam's anger was kindled, and he smote the ass with a staff" (Numbers 22:24-27 KJV).

viii. The mouth of the Ass was opened

The Lord is awesome in His wisdom. He opened the mouth of the Ass. This is an amazing knowledge. It is a good thing to know that God can open the mouth of His creation. No wonder they groan in pain for freedom.

"And the Lord opened the mouth of the ass, and she said unto Balaam, What have I done unto thee, that thou hast smitten me these three times? And Balaam said unto the ass, Because thou hast mocked me: I would there were a sword in mine hand, for now would I kill thee. And the ass said unto Balaam, Am not I thine ass, upon which thou hast ridden ever since I was thine unto this day? was I ever wont to do so unto thee? and he said, Nay. Then the Lord opened the eyes of Balaam, and he saw the angel of the Lord standing in the way, and his sword drawn in his hand: and he bowed down his head, and fell flat on his face. And the angel of the Lord said unto him, Wherefore hast thou smitten thine ass these three times? behold, I went out to withstand thee, because thy way is perverse before me: And the ass saw me, and turned from me these three times: unless she had turned from

me, surely now also I had slain thee, and saved her alive. And Balaam said unto the angel of the Lord, I have sinned; for I knew not that thou stoodest in the way against me: now therefore, if it displease thee, I will get me back again" (Numbers 22:28-34 KJV).

viii. The seas roar and the flood clap

When the sea roars, it is said to be nothing but a meaningless thing to a natural man, but I tell you the roaring of the sea can be a voice even a message undecoded. Who would have known that the floods have hands for clapping? Everything created by God is spiritual in their similitude.

"Let the sea roar, and the fulness thereof; the world, and they that dwell therein. Let the floods clap their hands: let the hills be joyful together" (Psalm 98:7-8 KJV).

God Can Speak Through Nature

God always seeks to help man. In an attempt to do so, He goes as far as using everything around a man to apprehend man's decision. He can speak to you through the most foolish things of the earth. Before the Lord can even open the mouths of the prophets, He might open the mouths of things that you consider inanimate to speak to you.

Oftentimes, people pray for months and days wanting to hear the voice of God. They want to receive God's direction about pertinent issues that surround them. They go on and on to pray but never receive a response. The truth is, God might have spoken but they were not paying attention. Did you observe that Balaam was just walking against the voice of God in the scripture? God was not going to give His permission with express vision but through the usage of the prophetic discernment that he has been taught by God. Even before Balaam's eyes were opened, God was already restraining Him using nature but he never discerned. God went as far as opening the mouth of the Ass yet Balaam still spoke to the Ass without fear. This was an Ass that had never spoken before. Until the Lord had to open Balaam's eyes before he knew the angel of the Lord's presence and operation around him.

"And the Lord opened the mouth of the ass, and she said unto Balaam, What have I done unto thee, that thou hast smitten me these three times? And Balaam said unto the ass, Because thou hast mocked me: I would there were a sword in mine hand, for now would I kill thee. And the ass said unto Balaam, Am not I thine ass, upon which thou hast ridden ever

since I was thine unto this day? was I ever wont to do so unto thee? and he said, Nay. Then the Lord opened the eyes of Balaam, and he saw the angel of the Lord standing in the way, and his sword drawn in his hand: and he bowed down his head, and fell flat on his face. And the angel of the Lord said unto him, Wherefore hast thou smitten thine ass these three times? behold, I went out to withstand thee, because thy way is perverse before me: And the ass saw me, and turned from me these three times: unless she had turned from me, surely now also I had slain thee, and saved her alive. And Balaam said unto the angel of the Lord, I have sinned; for I knew not that thou stoodest in the way against me: now therefore, if it displease thee, I will get me back again" (Numbers 22:28-34 KJV).

Operating in the Groaning Dimension of Tongues

The Lord wants to utter an inarticulate sound through us in the place of prayers. He wants us to operate like giants in life. He wants us to utter words in prayers beyond our weaknesses to pray and also hit the right note of the answer. This attempt of the spirit is what gives birth to groaning. How then can one operate in this dimension in the place of prayers?

1. Being Yielded to the Spirit of God:

The scripture says, "as many that are led by the spirit of God, are the sons of God" (Romans 8:14). Being led means one has to follow. The proof of being led is the following. You cannot be dictating the move and then claim to be led. Those who are led are only saddled with the responsibility of following. If the Spirit senses the need to groan, please follow.

2. Obedience to the Voice of God:

When the Spirit instructs groaning in your spirit, just follow. Don't rush out of the place of prayers.

"Whether it be good, or whether it be evil, we will obey the voice of the Lord our God, to whom we send thee; that it may be well with us, when we obey the voice of the Lord our God" (Jeremiah 42:6 KJV).

3. Hunger and Thirst:

There is a promise of God to pour His spirit upon all flesh in Joel 2:28. This promise is for all men. The secret to climbing higher on the ladder of this experience is hunger and thirst. If you push for it, you'll get it.

"For I will pour water upon him that is thirsty, and floods upon the dry ground: I will pour my spirit upon thy seed, and my blessing upon thine offspring: And they shall spring up as among the grass, as willows by the water courses. One shall say, I am the Lord's; and another shall call himself by the name of Jacob; and another shall subscribe with his hand unto the Lord, and surname himself by the name of Israel"
(Isaiah 44:3-5 KJV)

"Then Peter said unto them, Repent, and be baptized every one of you in the name of Jesus Christ for the remission of sins, and ye shall receive the gift of the Holy Ghost. For the promise is unto you, and to your children, and to all that are afar off, even as many as the Lord our God shall call" (Acts 2:38-39 KJV).

4. Consistency and Fervency In Praying In The Spirit:

There is a level of dedication that one needs to give to praying in tongues. This form of dedication comes with consistency; the degree of frequency. It is a burning desire to pray all the time in the spirit. This was Paul's testimony "I thank my God; I speak with tongues more than ye all" (1 Corinthians 14:18 KJV). If you are consistent, you will surely know and testify that you do just like Paul the Apostle. The human spirit needs to demonstrate this fervency of service regularly in conjunction with the Holy Spirit. "Not slothful in business; fervent in spirit; serving the Lord"(Romans 12:11).

5. Association With Intercessors:

Being in the company of men who are called intercessors is usually a plus to the prayer journey of any believer. The intercessors do more than groaning in the place of intercession. Imagine Saul who found Himself in the company of Prophets, he prophesied (1 Samuel 10:11). If you stay long enough there, you'll be like Jesus, groaning at the problem of people.

"He that walketh with wise men shall be wise: but a companion of fools shall be destroyed" (Proverbs 13:20).

Key Activation Prayers

Father in the name of Jesus, release the grace for the activation of this dimension upon me. Let your Holy Spirit groan in me and bring me to a place of mature intercessor. Open my ears and let me hear. Let me understand when you are trying to communicate to me through nature in Jesus' name. Amen!

Chapter

12

THE FOUR KINDS
OF BAPTISM

CHAPTER TWELVE

THE FOUR KINDS OF BAPTISM

"Then Peter said unto them, Repent, and be baptized every one of you in the name of Jesus Christ for the remission of sins, and ye shall receive the gift of the Holy Ghost. For the promise is unto you, and to your children, and to all that are afar off, even as many as the Lord our God shall call" (Acts 2:38-39 KJV).

Every believer needs to operate in this experience. The experience of baptism of the Holy Ghost is a promise to everyone just as the opening scripture affirmed. I love to describe the word baptism from the Latin word "baptizare" and from the Greek "baptizein" and "baptizo" meaning "immerse and dip in water", "dip repeatedly" "submerge", "make clean with water", and "overwhelm". It figuratively also means "be over one's head", and "to be soaked in wine".

Let us consider four kinds of baptism below:

1. Salvation baptism
This is a baptism into the name of Jesus. It is what qualifies the believer for the next stage of reality which is receiving the gift of the Holy Ghost.

"Then Peter said unto them, Repent, and be baptized every one of you in the name of Jesus Christ for the remission of sins, and ye shall receive the gift of the Holy Ghost" (Acts 2:38 KJV).

The blood of Jesus, the death, burial, and resurrection of Jesus testifies to the cleansing of the individual in this stage. It's the new birth experience where a believer confesses Jesus as his Lord and personal savior

"That if thou shalt confess with thy mouth the Lord Jesus, and shalt believe in thine heart that God hath raised him from the dead, thou shalt be saved. For with the heart man believeth unto righteousness; and with the mouth confession is made unto salvation" (Romans 10:9-10 KJV).

117

It is the beginning of the Journey. This is the point where the ministry of Jesus is being accepted. It is not the same as the Holy Ghost coming upon the believer with the evidence of speaking in tongues, but it opens the door for it.

> *"And it came to pass, that, while Apollos was at Corinth, Paul having passed through the upper coasts came to Ephesus: and finding certain disciples, He said unto them, Have ye received the Holy Ghost since ye believed? And they said unto him, We have not so much as heard whether there be any Holy Ghost. And he said unto them, Unto what then were ye baptized? And they said, Unto John's baptism. Then said Paul, John verily baptized with the baptism of repentance, saying unto the people, that they should believe on him which should come after him, that is, on Christ Jesus. When they heard this, they were baptized in the name of the Lord Jesus" (Acts 19:1-5 KJV).*

Here, the people who had John's baptism were converted into the baptism of Jesus' person; repentance, and believing in Christ Jesus. It is receiving the totality of Christ's sacrifice, and the revelation that He is the word of God (John 1:11-12). This is the code.

ii.   *Baptism with the gift of the Holy Ghost:*

After the first experience above, the second thing one will have to pray to experience is baptism with the gift of the Holy Ghost. In this case, the Holy Ghost becomes a gift to an individual. He fills the believers up. Hence, you will always see the scriptures say "they were filled with the Holy Ghost"

> *"And they were all filled with the Holy Ghost, and began to speak with other tongues, as the Spirit gave them utterance. And there were dwelling at Jerusalem Jews"*
> *(Acts 2:3-4KJV).*

Also, the Holy Ghost comes to bear witness of the saint's salvation through His abiding presence: *"The Spirit itself beareth witness with our spirit, that we are the children of God" (Romans 8:16)*. His introduction is usually with the evidence of speaking in tongues. Check what happened immediately after the salvation experience below.

> *"Then said Paul, John verily baptized with the baptism of repentance, saying unto the people, that they should believe on him which should come after him, that is, on Christ Jesus. When they heard this, they were baptized in the name of the Lord Jesus. And when Paul had laid his hands upon them, the Holy Ghost came on them; and they spake with tongues, and prophesied. And all the men were about twelve" (Acts 19:4-7 KJV).*

Did you observe that they were first baptized in the name of the Lord and then Paul laid his hands on them before the Holy Ghost came upon them? Peter also said repentance precedes baptism with the gift of the Holy Ghost.

"Then Peter said unto them, Repent, and be baptized every one of you in the name of Jesus Christ for the remission of sins, and ye shall receive the gift of the Holy Ghost. For the promise is unto you, and to your children, and to all that are afar off, even as many as the Lord our God shall call" (Acts 2:38-39 KJV).

The experience of some believers in Samaria below can help us to have a clearer understanding:

"But when they believed Philip preaching the things concerning the kingdom of God, and the name of Jesus Christ, they were baptized, both men and women. Then Simon himself believed also: and when he was baptized, he continued with Philip, and wondered, beholding the miracles and signs which were done. Now when the apostles which were at Jerusalem heard that Samaria had received the word of God, they sent unto them Peter and John: Who, when they were come down, prayed for them, that they might receive the Holy Ghost: (For as yet he was fallen upon none of them: only they were baptized in the name of the Lord Jesus.). Then laid they their hands on them, and they received the Holy Ghost" (Acts 8:12-17).

Did you notice that when the apostles who were at Jerusalem heard that Samaria had received the word of God, they sent unto them Peter and John? They received the word of God meant they gave their lives to Christ after preaching to them. Jesus is the word of God.

"He came unto his own, and his own received him not. But as many as received him, to them gave he power to become the sons of God, even to them that believe on his name" (John 1:11-12 KJV).

Did you also observe that the scripture clearly differentiated their experience as limited to only being baptized in the name of the Lord and that the Holy Ghost had fallen on none of them? See it here in "vs. 16-17" *"Who, when they were come down, prayed for them, that they might receive the Holy Ghost: (For as yet he was fallen upon none of them: only they were baptized in the name of the Lord Jesus.). Then laid they their hands on them, and they received the Holy Ghost"*

The experience of being baptized usually comes with the laying on of hands or individual waiting on the Lord and prayers for the baptism. In the above scripture, Paul laid his hands, but in some other scripture Peter only spoke words and the Holy Ghost fell.

"While Peter yet spake these words, the Holy Ghost fell on all them which heard the word. And they of the circumcision which believed were astonished, as many as came with Peter, because that on the Gentiles also was poured out the gift of the Holy Ghost. For they heard them speak with tongues, and magnify God. Then answered Peter Can any man forbid water, that these should not be baptized, which have received the Holy Ghost as well as we? And he commanded them to be baptized in the name of the Lord. Then prayed they him to tarry certain days" (Acts 10:44-48 KJV).

iii.   Water Baptism

Water baptism is a subsequent salvation experience. After one has received Jesus, and has been baptized with the Holy Ghost with the evidence of speaking with tongues, next is water baptism.

"For they heard them speak with tongues, and magnify God. Then answered Peter Can any man forbid water, that these should not be baptized, which have received the Holy Ghost as well as we? And he commanded them to be baptized in the name of the Lord. Then prayed they him to tarry certain days" (Acts 10:44-48 KJV).

Although, there are cases where individuals might have to be baptized with water immediately after receiving Jesus. Always note that the most important is that they must receive Jesus before being baptized in the water or in the Holy Ghost.

"And as they went on their way, they came unto a certain water: and the eunuch said, See, here is water; what doth hinder me to be baptized? And Philip said, If thou believest with all thine heart, thou mayest. And he answered and said, I believe that Jesus Christ is the Son of God" (Acts 8:36-37 KJV).

Did you observe that before Philip baptized the Eunuch, He led him to Christ? This is exactly what I am talking about. The type of water baptism conducted as seen above is a full immersion into water.

iv.   Continuous Baptism of the Holy Ghost

This is a post-salvation and post-water baptism experience. It is a continuous filling of the Holy Ghost. An experience that is meant for everyone born of the Spirit, and in earnest expectation of spiritual growth. Every believer can go by the highlight of the Apostles' waiting in the upper room during the feast of Pentecost to receive the consequent baptism of the Holy Ghost which is seen as the first necessary empowerment for running the Christian race.

> *"And there appeared unto them cloven tongues like as of fire, and it sat upon each of them. And they were all filled with the Holy Ghost and began to speak with other tongues, as the Spirit gave them utterance" (Acts 2:3-4 KJV).*

Moreover, the Apostles of Jesus desired more than a one-time experience of being filled with the Holy Ghost. This is evident in their subsequent fellowship with God. This evident fact was nothing but proof that they had the full knowledge of the necessity of the Holy Ghost in their daily walk as they could not do without Him. We saw this again when they were soon confronted with challenges as they carried out their mandated duty. Quickly they assembled, and when they did, they were all filled again.

> *"When they had prayed, the place was shaken where they were assembled together; and they were all filled with the Holy Ghost, and they spake the word of God with boldness" (Acts 4:31).*

Owing to this, we were all admonished in Ephesians 5:18… *"And be not drunk with wine, wherein is excess; but be filled with the Spirit"*. The continuous infilling of the Spirit helps us to walk worthy in the Spirit. We are being empowered again and again to take charge and overturn the darts of the enemies that he might unleash against us.

The Promise Is For Everyone In Christ

God's desire and plan is that everyone might receive the promise of the Holy Spirit. Peter shows us how to go about it. He reiterated the prophecy of Prophet Joel and then added the imperative point for receiving the gift which is repentance.

> *"And it shall come to pass in the last days, saith God, I will pour out of my Spirit upon all flesh: and your sons and your daughters shall prophesy, and your young men shall see visions, and your old men shall dream dreams. Then Peter said unto them, Repent,*

*and be baptized every one of you in the name of Jesus Christ for the remission of sins,
and ye shall receive the gift of the Holy Ghost. For the promise is unto you, and to your
children, and to all that are afar off, even as many as the Lord our God shall call "(Acts
2:17, 38-39KJV).*

Another thing we need to look at is the instruction of Jesus to His disciples. It is something
we need to glean from. Carefully look at what Jesus told His disciples

*"And I will pray the Father, and he shall give you another Comforter, that he may abide
with you for ever; Even the Spirit of truth; whom the world cannot receive, because it
seeth him not, neither knoweth him: but ye know him; for he dwelleth with you, and shall
be in you. But the Comforter, which is the Holy Ghost, whom the Father will send in my
name, he shall teach you all things, and bring all things to your remembrance,
whatsoever I have said unto you" (John 14:16-17, 26).*

Consequently, Jesus came back to them in Acts 20:20-22
*"And when he had so said, he shewed unto them his hands and his side. Then were the
disciples glad, when they saw the Lord. Then said Jesus to them again, Peace be unto you: as
my Father hath sent me, even so send I you. And when he had said this, he breathed on them,
and saith unto them, Receive ye the Holy Ghost ".*

He breathed upon them the Holy Ghost of promise in this chapter, to fulfill what He told
them previously in John 14 above saying "Even *the Spirit of truth; whom the world cannot
receive, because it seeth him not, neither knoweth him: but ye know him; for he dwelleth with
you, and shall be in you ".* Jesus was the one that had been with them. It is His Spirit that shall
now be in them according to the promise; the Holy Ghost. Therefore, Jesus blew on them
His breath and His Spirit; the Holy Ghost. This experience was only for the foundational
Apostles. However, Jesus told them to tarry again at Jerusalem for the enduement of power
at the invasion of the Holy Ghost (Acts 1:8).

Every other person who was not there when Jesus initially blew on the foundational
disciples at the first invasion of the Holy Ghost in John 20:20-22 had the opportunity of
being filled in Acts 2:2-4 which is the second invasion of the Holy Ghost. Acts 2:1-4 does not
depict the first invasion of the Holy Spirit to the earth. The book of Acts 1:8 was a promise of
infilling of power for those who had received the Holy Ghost initially in John 20:22.
However, it was a first-time experience for others.

Baptism and The Similitude of the Holy Spirit in The Old Testament

The Holy Spirit was well represented in the journey of the Israelites. He carried them throughout their journeys. He guided them. He supplied all their needs. The Holy Spirit achieved everything He did in the Old Testament in a figure. The reason for that was that not many of them had personal knowledge of Him but just a few that were chosen by God. Although they saw His acts, He showed His ways to Moses (Psalms 103:7). The one He showed His ways is different from the one who knew His acts alone

"In all their affliction he was afflicted, and the angel of his presence saved them: in his love and in his pity he redeemed them, and he bare them, and carried them all the days of old. But they rebelled, and vexed his Holy Spirit: therefore, he was turned to be their enemy, and he fought against them" (Isaiah 63:9-10).

Also, the experiences of certain men in the Old Testament were as though they walked in the New Testament. The Holy Spirit walked with a few of them with considerable exemptions. The rule of the law could not confine His presence to an ark. Although, the law was present as a witness in some cases, yet the Spirit behind the law still gave certain exemptions. The express description of the person of the Holy Spirit and His full invasion was a promise for the believers of Christ in the New Testament. Nevertheless, a dimension of this fenced-up truth was witnessed in the lives of some men in the Old Testament. These men walked in the Spirit. Enoch's translation cannot be ignored till date. The scripture has the testimony that He walked with God and was translated so that He would not see death. Have you ever asked yourself? How did Enoch walk with God? God is a Spirit (John 4:24). Enoch walked with the Spirit.

"And Enoch walked with God: and he was not; for God took him" (Genesis 5:24).
"By faith Enoch was translated that he should not see death; and was not found, because God had translated him: for before his translation he had this testimony, that he pleased God."

Before the law was introduced, Abraham walked with God. He was called the father of faith. He was one of the patriarchs who enjoyed the rarest theophanic manifestation of God. I mean God literarily ate physical food with Him many times:

"And the Lord appeared unto him in the plains of Mamre: and he sat in the tent door in the heat of the day; And he lift up his eyes and looked, and, lo, three men stood by him:

and when he saw them, he ran to meet them from the tent door, and bowed himself toward the ground, And said, My Lord, if now I have found favour in thy sight, pass not away, I pray thee, from thy servant: Let a little water, I pray you, be fetched, and wash your feet, and rest yourselves under the tree: And I will fetch a morsel of bread, and comfort ye your hearts; after that ye shall pass on: for therefore are ye come to your servant. And they said, So do, as thou hast said. And Abraham hastened into the tent unto Sarah, and said, Make ready quickly three measures of fine meal, knead it, and make cakes upon the hearth. And Abraham ran unto the herd, and fetcht a calf tender and good, and gave it unto a young man; and he hasted to dress it. And he took butter, and milk, and the calf which he had dressed, and set it before them; and he stood by them under the tree, and they did eat" (Genesis 18:1-8KJV)

"And Melchizedek king of Salem brought forth bread and wine: and he was the priest of the most high God. And he blessed him, and said, Blessed be Abram of the most high God, possessor of heaven and earth"(Genesis 14:18-20).

This kind of communion was a deep one. These men had a better understanding of God. Furthermore, let us examine baptism and the walk of the Holy Spirit in the Old Testament under the three sub-headings below:

1.   Baptism Into the Cloud

The Bible gave a testimony that God carried the Israelites all the days of old. How did He do it? It was through the pillar of fire and the pillar of cloud. He led them throughout the days of old and fought for them through it. Notwithstanding, He still fought with them when they rebelled against Him.

"In all their affliction he was afflicted, and the angel of his presence saved them: in his love and in his pity he redeemed them, and he bare them, <u>and carried them all the days of old</u>. But they rebelled, and vexed his holy Spirit: therefore, he was turned to be their enemy, and he fought against them" (Isaiah 63:9-10).

The pillar of fire, cloud, and glory was the popular theophanic manifestation of God in the days of Moses. Its regular appearance was awestriking. This was the atmosphere that introduced God's presence to the people. It was so magnificent. God did not manifest this dimension of Glory to some Patriarchs but He did to Moses. It was a completely different theophanic manifestation of God.

"And it came to pass, as Moses entered into the tabernacle, the cloudy pillar descended, and stood at the door of the tabernacle, and the Lord talked with Moses. And all the people saw the cloudy pillar stand at the tabernacle door: and all the people rose up and worshipped, every man in his tent door" (Exodus 33:9-10 KJV).

The descent of the cloudy pillar in the days of Moses was usually a determinant of the people's worship. It was a sign that indicated God's perception of their sacrifices. It was an indicator of God's presence in the Tabernacle or on the mountain. The people were literally absorbed into Moses in the cloud. Moses was their spokesman before God. Whatever happened through the cloud of glory and the pillar of fire to the Israelites was a decision of Moses' fellowship. He was the intercessor and mediator of the people before the Lord. Moses literally carried all the Israelites into the cloud through the burdens he bore. This is why the scripture says *"moreover, brethren, I would not that ye should be ignorant, how that all our fathers were under the cloud, and all passed through the sea; And were all baptized unto Moses in the cloud and in the sea" (1 Corinthians 10:1-2KJV).*

The Tabernacle of congregation was persistently in expectation of the descent of the cloud of glory. God's presence was always registered on the Tabernacle of congregation in the form of the cloud of glory from time to time as often as there was genuine worship unto God.

"Then a cloud covered the tent of the congregation, and the glory of the Lord filled the tabernacle. And Moses was not able to enter into the tent of the congregation, because the cloud abode thereon, and the glory of the Lord filled the tabernacle "(Exodus 40:34-35).

Anyone who entered into the house of the Lord knew that they would see the pillar of fire and cloud of glory as a consequent experience of offering genuine sacrifices unto God. One of the duties of the pillar of fire is that it creates the cloud of glory amid genuine worship. In the days of Solomon, it was the fire that came from heaven that created the cloud of glory. This is why I say the pillar of fire is the theophanic manifestation of God. It was self-divisive into the pillar of cloud and the cloud of glory.

"Now when Solomon had made an end of praying, the fire came down from heaven, and consumed the burnt offering and the sacrifices; and the glory of the Lord filled the house. And the priests could not enter into the house of the Lord, because the glory of the Lord had filled the Lord's house. And when all the children of Israel saw how the fire came

125

down, and the glory of the Lord upon the house, they bowed themselves with their faces to the ground upon the pavement, and worshipped, and praised the Lord, saying, For he is good; for his mercy endureth for ever" (2 Chronicles 7:1-3).

Moreover, God led the Israelites in all their journeys. This is exactly the purpose of the Spirit of the Lord in the New Testament. The Holy Spirit leads the Sons of God; the believers of Christ (Romans 8:14). The pillar of cloud was a frequent symbol of direction for the Israelites. It was the vital evidence that they would get to the promise land and not miss their way.

"And the Lord went before them by day in a pillar of a cloud, to lead them the way; and by night in a pillar of fire, to give them light; to go by day and night: He took not away the pillar of the cloud by day, nor the pillar of fire by night, from before the people" (Exodus 13:21-22).

"And when the cloud was taken up from over the tabernacle, the children of Israel went onward in all their journeys: But if the cloud were not taken up, then they journeyed not till the day that it was taken up. For the cloud of the Lord was upon the tabernacle by day, and fire was on it by night, in the sight of all the house of Israel, throughout all their journeys "(Exodus 40:34-38).

2.   Baptism Into the Water

Water baptism is an immersion into water. The key experience of baptism is the soaking and submersion into the water. The purpose of water baptism is cleansing. It is a form of the witness of God on earth for mankind's salvation both in the Old and the New Testament.

"For there are three that bear record in heaven, the Father, the Word, and the Holy Ghost: and these three are one" (1 John 5:7).

In the Old Testament, water was used for ceremonial cleansing. It was a symbol of new life, redemption, and salvation. Moses was like the custodian of the cleansing dimension for His generation. The figure of sprinkling began to find expression little by little in the days of Moses. The Mosaic law revealed so much about cleansing through the water and the blood. It was used consistently in matters of violations. It was administered through sprinkling and self-washing. God practically instructed the washing of the water to Moses, a requirement for wholeness and victory over sin and transgressions.

> *"Whosoever toucheth the dead body of any man that is dead, and purifieth not himself, defileth the tabernacle of the Lord; and that soul shall be cut off from Israel: because the water of separation was not sprinkled upon him, he shall be unclean; his uncleanness is yet upon him" (Numbers 19:13).*

Water was used for other various reasons in the Old Testament. It was used as a symbol for the outpouring of the Spirit upon the thirsty soul and ground.

> *"For I will pour water upon him that is thirsty, and floods upon the dry ground: I will pour my spirit upon thy seed, and my blessing upon thine offspring" (Isaiah 44:3).*

It was a symbol of the depths and dimensions of salvation that comes from the Lord to His people.

> *"Therefore, with joy shall ye draw water out of the wells of salvation" (Isaiah 12:3).*
> *" For my people have committed two evils; they have forsaken me the fountain of living waters, and hewed them out cisterns, broken cisterns, that can hold no water " (Jeremiah 2:13).*

The Mosaic law was aggressive toward the Israelites because it does not make a provision for an oversight. Violators of the laws were instantly killed by God in some cases, while others were redeemed by following the ceremonial laws of redemption. The use of water in a ceremonial way for atonement was one of God's popular and effective ways of bringing solutions to the problems of filthiness. When the people passed through the red sea on dry ground, the conclusion of their experience was described as baptism.

> *"Moreover, brethren, I would not that ye should be ignorant, how that all our fathers were under the cloud, and all passed through the sea; And were all baptized unto Moses in the cloud and in the sea" (1 Corinthians 10:1-2KJV).*

Hence, passing through the red sea was a form of water baptism. A symbol of salvation for the Israelites, and a tip of judgment for the enemies; the Egyptians.

3.   *Baptism of The Spirit*

Diverse people experienced God in several ways in the Old Testament. They saw God and His Holy Spirit in some forms. The Bible clearly tells us that the church in the Old Testament walked with the Holy Spirit. Who would have imagined that the Holy Spirit was the one that carried the Israelites throughout the days of Old if not that the Bible said it? The next question is how did they walk with Him?

"In all their affliction he was afflicted, and the angel of his presence saved them: in his love and in his pity, he redeemed them; and he bare them, and carried them all the days of old. But they rebelled, and vexed his holy Spirit: therefore, he was turned to be their enemy, and he fought against them" (Isaiah 63:9 KJV).

The Holy Spirit of God was the angel of God's presence that redeemed His Children in the Old Testament. The scripture said He bore them and carried them throughout the Old Testament. Besides this, David was another man whom the scripture declared to have the Holy Spirit. While David was praying, He said, *"Cast me not away from thy presence; and take not thy holy spirit from me".* This means David had the Holy Spirit, and he enjoyed the Holy Spirit's benefit in some way.

In the New Testament, there are gifts mentioned as the gifts of the Spirit. Prophecy and the working of miracles are a part of them. Relating the manifestation of the Holy Spirit in the Old Testament to that of the New, one would see the oneness of operation.

"To another the working of miracles; to another prophecy; to another discerning of spirits; to another divers kind of tongues; to another the interpretation of tongues" (1 Corinthians 12:10).

"And the Lord came down in a cloud, and spake unto him, and took of the spirit that was upon him, and gave it unto the seventy elders: and it came to pass, that, when the spirit rested upon them, they prophesied, and did not cease" (Numbers 11:24).
"And when Paul had laid his hands upon them, the Holy Ghost came on them; and they spake with tongues, and prophesied" (Acts 19:6).

Moses operated in the dimension of the Holy Spirit upon him. He had the gifts of prophecy, working of miracles, and so on operating in his life. The reaction that took place suddenly after God took from the Spirit upon him and gave it to the seventy is that they prophesied.

This experience was synonymous with the experience of the disciples of Jesus and others who received the Holy Spirit and His evidence. They prophesied.

The Spirit Within

There is a ministry of the Spirit within and the Spirit upon in the New and the Old Testament. The presence of the Holy Spirit was with David. According to the scripture, David said *"Create in me a pure heart, O God, and renew a steadfast spirit within me. Do not cast me from your presence or take your Holy Spirit from me" (Psalm 51:10-11 NIV)*. This is the testimony that David had the Holy Spirit.

Daniel also had the Spirit within. The scripture gave the testimony was in Him. Part of the operation of the Holy Spirit in Daniel was the operation of the word of wisdom and the gift of interpretation.

"There is a man in thy kingdom, <u>in whom is the spirit of the holy gods</u>; and in the days of thy father light and understanding and wisdom, like the wisdom of the gods, was found in him; whom the king Nebuchadnezzar thy father, the king, I say, thy father, made master of the magicians, astrologers, Chaldeans, and soothsayers; I have even heard of thee, <u>that the spirit of the gods is in thee</u>, and that light and understanding and excellent wisdom is found in thee" (Daniel 5:11,14).

Furthermore, let us see what Jesus said to His believers on what to do with the ministry of the Holy Spirit "within" in the New Testament.

"And I will ask the Father, and he will give you another advocate to help you and be with you forever— the Spirit of truth. The world cannot accept him, because it neither sees him nor knows him. But you know him, for he lives with you and will be in you" (John 14:16-17 NIV).

"As for you, the anointing you received from him remains in you, and you do not need anyone to teach you. But as his anointing teaches you about all things and as that anointing is real, not counterfeit—just as it has taught you, remain in him" (1 John 2:27 NIV).

The Spirit within was the anointing within. He was to teach them, guide them and comfort them.

The Spirit Upon

The power and the dimensions of the gift were evident manifestations in the Old and the New Testaments. It was referred to as the working of the Spirit "upon".

Many people in the Old Testament walked in the dimension of the Spirit "Upon". See the list of a few people according to the scriptures:

I. Othniel the son of Kenaz, Caleb's younger brother

    "And the Spirit of the Lord came upon him, and he judged Israel and went out to war: and the Lord delivered Chushanrishathaim king of Mesopotamia into his hand; and his hand prevailed against Chushanrishathaim" (Judges 3:10).

ii. Gideon

    "But the Spirit of the Lord came upon Gideon, and he blew a trumpet; and Abiezer was gathered after him" (Judges 6:34)

iii. Jephtha

    "Then the Spirit of the Lord came on Jephthah. He crossed Gilead and Manasseh, passed through Mizpah of Gilead, and from there he advanced against the Ammonites" (Judges 11:29).

iv. Samson

    "The Spirit of the Lord came powerfully upon him so that he tore the lion apart with his bare hands as he might have torn a young goat. But he told neither his father nor his mother what he had done" (Judges 14:6)

v. Ezekiel

    "And the Spirit of the Lord fell upon me, and said unto me, Speak; Thus saith the Lord; Thus have ye said, O house of Israel: for I know the things that come into your mind, every one of them" (Ezekiel 11:5 KJV)

All these people experienced "the Spirit Upon" dimension of the Holy Spirit. They prophesied, walked in might, wisdom, and did many mighty things for the Lord. Each of these operations of "the Spirit upon" in the New Testament is what is now called "the gift" of the Holy Spirit.

Key Activation Prayers

Awesome Holy Spirit, come upon me with your fresh baptism and the fire to operate in the dimension of tongues continually. Release the burning fire upon me. Activate this dimension right now in Jesus' name. Amen!

Chapter

13

THE MISAPPREHENSION ABOUT SPEAKING IN TONGUES

CHAPTER THIRTEEN

THE MISAPPREHENSION ABOUT SPEAKING IN TONGUES

"Charity never faileth: but whether there be prophecies, they shall fail; whether there be tongues, they shall cease; whether there be knowledge, it shall vanish away. For we know in part, and we prophesy in part. But when that which is perfect is come, then that which is in part shall be done away" (1 Corinthians 13:8-10 KJV).

There are lots of criticisms that surround the subject of speaking in tongues. Too many people don't believe in speaking in tongues for some reason. Some of the reasons deterring people from speaking in tongues do not usually hold water. Many of the people who don't see speaking in tongues as an important gift of the Spirit either do so because they were told something negative about it or they had a wrong perception. The misconceptions of certain scriptures are major introductions of the cause and effect of the arguments about speaking in an unknown tongue. Over the years, we have seen diverse arguments on the subject of speaking in tongues. Some of the arguments remain in the hearts of people till date. A few of them will be listed below as they are being debated regularly:

1.   The statement "No more unknown tongues, they have ceased".
This criticism is from the misconception of the scripture. The scripture that is usually taken out of context is:

"Charity never faileth: but whether there be prophecies, they shall fail; whether there be tongues, they shall cease; whether there be knowledge, it shall vanish away. For we know in part, and we prophesy in part. But when that which is perfect is come, then that which is in part shall be done away" (1 Corinthians 13:8-10 KJV).

Looking at the text, you'll see that it is never talking about now, but when we shall be face to face with the Lord. This is what it means to say "when that which is perfect is come". This is the reason Paul further said

"When I was a child, I spake as a child, I understood as a child, I thought as a child: but when I became a man, I put away childish things. For now we see through a glass, darkly; but then face to face: now I know in part; but then shall I know even as also I am known".

His affirmation to have grown to being a man now and being able to successfully put away childish things instructs the mind about the tense of his experience. Furthermore, what do you think would have made him say "We see through a dark glass now, but then expecting to see face to face?" The answer is the anticipation of life beyond this world, the final appearance of Christ, the joy and expectation of every man born of God.

2.   The statement "Jesus never at any time spoke in tongues".
Jesus never spoke in tongues is the usual claim of this misapprehension. Nevertheless, the glorification of His spirit was what ushered in the baptism of the Holy Spirit, and manifestation with the evidence of speaking in tongues. Speaking in tongues is a gift and evidence of the Holy Spirit. However, the Interpretation of tongues is the prophecy of an unknown tongue. The Holy Spirit is the "In Him" that was promised to be "In Us". He is the spirit of the resurrected Jesus; the third person of the Godhead. If speaking in tongues is the evidence of the spirit then an unknown tongue is the language of Jesus because the Holy Spirit is His Spirit.

Moreover, you need to know that an unknown tongue is a voice expression undecoded. It's a language that is only known in the Spirit. An example of what this can look like is demonstrated below, a Chinese man stands before a Briton to speak Mandarin, he'll definitely make no sense except the Briton is learned in the language or if he gets an interpreter. "For he that speaketh in an unknown tongue speaketh not unto men, but unto God: for no man understandeth him; howbeit in the spirit he speaketh mysteries" (1 Corinthians 14:2 KJV). Communication is always channeled towards making the listener(s) understand the message. If the listener does not understand the message, then there is a breach of communication. This is the principle of communication and the use of language. An unknown tongue is a "yet-to-be-interpreted voice". Let's learn from the mystery coding demystified by Jesus. This is nothing but an unknown voice that needed to be interpreted by Him:

"Father, glorify thy name. Then came there a voice from heaven, saying, I have both glorified it, and will glorify it again. Father, glorify thy name. Then came there a voice from heaven, saying, I have both glorified it, and will glorify it again. <u>The people</u>

therefore, that stood by, and heard it, said that it thundered: others said, An angel spake to him. Jesus answered and said, this voice came not because of me, but for your sakes. Now is the judgment of this world: now shall the prince of this world be cast out. And I, if I be lifted up from the earth, will draw all men unto me. This he said, signifying what death he should die" (John 12:28-33).

The Bible calls the above a voice, yet it was just like thunder with no specific understanding to the people. They heard it but could not discern what it means.

Some said an angel spoke with Jesus but they had no specific understanding of what was said. This means that the voice was implicit. Only the person with understanding would know the interpretation of the thunderous voice. The Bible affirmed the above that Jesus answered and said, This voice came not because of me, but for your sakes. The implication of what the people called "the thunderous voice" was the significance of both the emancipation of the people and the judgment of the god of this world through the nature of death, that Jesus was to die for mankind. Hearing and understanding the tongue is a sign that Jesus is familiar with any deity's language. He knows what an unknown tongue is like. In fact, the unknown tongue is a voice of His spirit. According to the scripture, an unknown tongue is like a stammering tongue:

"For with stammering lips and another tongue will he speak to this people. To whom he said, this is the rest wherewith ye may cause the weary to rest; and this is the refreshing: yet they would not hear" (Isaiah 28:11-12).

The unknown tongue is Jesus speaking through those who believe in Him. We can only speak in His name and not without His name. Speaking in an unknown tongue is a provision made available in the name of Jesus:

"And these signs shall follow them that believe; In my name shall they cast out devils; they shall speak with new tongues" (Mark 16:17).

Groaning is a dimension already explained in this book. Jesus groaned in the spirit at the tomb of Lazarus. He groaned to express His request concerning the death of Lazarus.

"When Jesus, therefore, saw her weeping, and the Jews also weeping which came with her, he <u>groaned in the spirit</u> and was troubled. Jesus therefore again groaning in himself cometh to the grave. It was a cave, and a stone lay upon it" (John 11:33, 38).

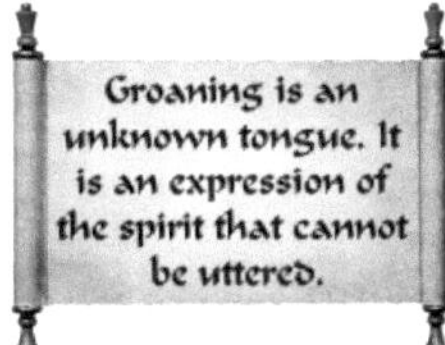

The groaning of Jesus was an expression of His dissatisfaction about the death of Lazarus. He groaned in Himself while moving towards the grave. Jesus made groanings that cannot be uttered in meaningful words, except it is being interpreted by men with the gift of speaking in tongues and interpretation. Groaning is an unknown tongue. It is an expression of the spirit that cannot be uttered:

"Likewise the Spirit also helpeth our infirmities: for we know not what we should pray for as we ought: but the Spirit itself maketh intercession for us with groanings which cannot be uttered" (Romans 8: 26).

Jesus practically spoke in the spirit by groaning. This is a leap into the New Testament experience. It happened a while before it became a public benefit. Hence, everyone that speaks in tongues afterward can only do so because of the resurrection of Jesus. His Holy Spirit has been sent to us who believe in Him. He now speaks to us with stammering tongues.

"For with stammering lips and another tongue will he speak to this people. To whom he said, this is the rest wherewith ye may cause the weary to rest; and this is the refreshing: yet they would not hear" (Isaiah 28:11-12).

3.   The statement "tongue is from the devil".
Speaking in tongues is a promise of God to His ward. It is His promise in the New Testament to all who believe in Christ. It is never from the devil. This is why the scripture says:

"If a son shall ask bread of any of you that is a father, will he give him a stone? or if he ask a fish, will he for a fish give him a serpent? Or if he shall ask an egg, will he offer him a scorpion? If ye then, being evil, know how to give good gifts unto your children: how much more shall your heavenly Father give the Holy Spirit to them that ask him?" (Luke 11:11-13).

The scripture used by Jesus above is about the welfare of the son in a relationship with the father. No such child would ask for a bread and get a stone. Neither would he ask for a fish and then get a serpent instead. The father would never even give the child a scorpion instead of an egg. Hence, God will not give anything of the devil to us in place of the Holy Spirit. Speaking in tongues is a gift from the Holy Spirit. It is not a gift from the devil.

4.   The statement "Only the foundational Apostles and others with the gift of office can speak in tongues".

The promise of speaking in tongues is for all believers. However, not too many have harnessed the spiritual spigot. Everyone who is not yet working in the reality of speaking in tongues can do so, even now.

The scripture says even if you don't speak in tongues, you can covet it.

> *"Are all apostles? are all prophets? are all teachers? are all workers of miracles? Have all the gifts of healing? do all speak with tongues? do all interpret? But covet earnestly the best gifts: and yet shew I unto you a more excellent way"*
> *(1 Corinthians 12:29-31KJV).*

The word of the Lord spoken through prophet Joel lets us know that the outpouring of the Spirit is for everyone "all flesh, your sons and your daughters".

> *"And it shall come to pass in the last days, saith God, I will pour out of my Spirit upon all flesh: and your sons and your daughters shall prophesy, and your young men shall see visions, and your old men shall dream dreams"*
> *(Acts 2:17 KJV).*

The Apostles of Christ experienced this. They spoke in tongues and their tongues became prophecies through the angelic interpretation of tongues to the hearers. This was how tongues became prophecies through angelic interpretation.

> *"And they were all filled with the Holy Ghost, and began to speak with other tongues, as the Spirit gave them utterance. And there were dwelling at Jerusalem Jews, devout men, out of every nation under heaven. Now when this was noised abroad, the multitude came together, and were confounded, because that every man heard them speak in his own language. And they were all amazed and marvelled, saying one to another, Behold, are not all these which speak Galilaeans? And how hear we every man in our own tongue, wherein we were born?" (Acts 2:4-8).*

Speaking in tongues is the promise of God to every believer in Christ Jesus. It is not for only the Apostles and other men with any gift of office in the body of Christ.

"And these signs shall follow them that believe; In my name shall they cast out devils; they shall speak with new tongues" (Mark 16:17 KJV).

5.   The statement "One cannot speak in tongues at will".

Prayer is more of a man's desire than it is the regular Spirit's push. Whether the spirit impresses it or not, man is supposed to pray without ceasing. This is what Jesus said.

"And he spake a parable unto them to this end, that men ought always to pray, and not to faint; Saying, There was in a city a judge, which feared not God, neither regarded man: And there was a widow in that city; and she came unto him, saying, Avenge me of mine adversary. And he would not for a while: but afterward he said within himself, Though I fear not God, nor regard man; Yet because this widow troubleth me, I will avenge her, lest by her continual coming she weary me" (Luke 18:1-5 KJV).

The scripture says "man ought always to pray" and not "man ought to be pushed to pray". This means the desire to pray has to be superimposed in the will of man always. It should be a regular burning desire. *"Therefore, I say unto you, What things soever ye desire, when ye pray, believe that ye receive them, and ye shall have them" (Mark 11:24 KJV).*

Did you observe the word "desire" in the above verse? This desire is your will and your wish.

Again, Jesus said "If ye abide in me, and my words abide in you, ye shall ask what ye will, and it shall be done unto you" (John 15:7 KJV). Jesus said if you abide in Him, He'll grant you your will. Hence, Paul said "What is it then? <u>I will pray with the spirit</u>, and <u>I will pray</u> with the understanding also: <u>I will sing with the spirit</u>, and I will sing with the understanding also" (1 Corinthians 14:15). This statement means My prayer in the spirit can be my will. It is me operating the gift as seen from the word "I will pray". I can subject the operation of this gift to my apt desire and will at any time when I sense the need to pray. It means an unknown tongue can come out of my mouth at will. I don't have to wait for some strange force to come upon me before I pray in an unknown tongue. I will pray with the spirit always. Now that I have the gift, I can pray at will.

6.   The statement "No salvation without baptism in the Holy Spirit with the evidence of speaking in tongues".

When one gets born again, such a person is sealed with the evidence of salvation in Christ Jesus. This is called baptism into the name of the Lord Jesus. This does not require the baptism of the Holy Spirit and evidence of speaking in tongues. This is purely a baptism into the name of the Lord Jesus with the testimony of the washing of His blood.

"Then said Paul, John verily baptized with the baptism of repentance, saying unto the people, that they should believe on him which should come after him, that is, on Christ Jesus. When they heard this, they were baptized in the name of the Lord Jesus.

And when Paul had laid his hands upon them, the Holy Ghost came on them; and they spake with tongues, and prophesied. And all the men were about twelve" (Acts 19:4-7).

Moreover, after Paul had laid His hands on them, the Holy Ghost came upon them, then they spoke in tongues and prophesied. There is a clear difference between the two experiences. In one experience, confession was done as they were baptized into the person of Jesus. In the other experience, Paul's hands were laid on them so that they would receive the Holy Ghost. Their salvation was never predicated on receiving the Holy Ghost and Speaking in tongues first, but on believing. This is why the scripture says "In whom ye also trusted, after that ye heard the word of truth, the gospel of your salvation: in whom also after that ye believed, ye were sealed with that holy Spirit of promise" (Ephesians 1:13 KJV). The Holy Spirit witnesses His seal upon a believer after such a believer has received and accepted the gospel of Christ.

7.   The statement that "speaking in tongues means speaking someone's native tongue". When one prays in tongues, He does not speak to any man, but unto God. He speaks mysteries in the Spirit. If He does not speak to man, then He does not speak any man's language. It is the spirit's praying.

"For he that speaketh in an unknown tongue speaketh not unto men, but unto God: for no man understandeth him; howbeit in the spirit he speaketh mysteries. For if I pray in an unknown tongue, my spirit prayeth, but my understanding is unfruitful" (1 Corinthians 14:2, 14 KJV).

Notwithstanding, it is important to know that the Spirit can give the interpretation of any tongue in any language, either directly by Himself or through the individuals who possess the gifts of tongue interpretation. This was what happened on the day of Pentecost while they were in one accord in the upper room waiting for the promise of the Spirit. The Holy

Ghost opened the ears of their listeners. He gave them interpretations and understanding.

"And they were all filled with the Holy Ghost, and began to speak with other tongues, as the Spirit gave them utterance. And there were dwelling at Jerusalem Jews, devout men, out of every nation under heaven. Now when this was noised abroad, the multitude came together, and were confounded, because that every man heard them speak in his own language. And they were all amazed and marvelled, saying one to another, Behold, are not all these which speak Galilaeans? And how hear we every man in our own tongue, wherein we were born? Parthians, and Medes, and Elamites, and the dwellers in Mesopotamia, and in Judaea, and Cappadocia, in Pontus, and Asia, Phrygia, and Pamphylia, in Egypt, and in the parts of Libya about Cyrene, and strangers of Rome, Jews and proselytes, Cretes and Arabians, we do hear them speak in our tongues the wonderful works of God. And they were all amazed, and were in doubt, saying one to another, What meaneth this? (Acts 2:4-12 KJV).

The whole of the people that gathered at the fame of what was happening heard the disciples in their native tongues. Everyone from every nation heard them speak the wonderful works of God. They all heard the same thing. Don't forget that the disciples were only speaking in tongues. Who was doing the interpretation? It was the Holy Ghost! The angels of interpretation were giving them the meaning of what was being said. They received the tongues as prophecy. What was the prophecy the listeners received? It was the interpretation "the wonderful works of God". Tongues with interpretation is prophecy. "I would that ye all spake with tongues but rather that ye prophesied: for greater is he that prophesieth than he that speaketh with tongues, except he interprets, that the church may receive edifying (1 Corinthians 14:5 KJV). Prophecy is for church edification, and tongue is meant for self-edification. The moment an unknown tongue is interpreted it becomes prophecy.

"While the listeners were confounded about what they heard, Peter stood up lifted up his voice, and said unto them, Ye men of Judaea, and all ye that dwell at Jerusalem, be this known unto you, and hearken to my words: For these are not drunken, as ye suppose, seeing it is but the third hour of the day. But this is that which was spoken by the prophet Joel; And it shall come to pass in the last days, saith God, I will pour out of my Spirit upon all flesh: and your sons and your daughters shall prophesy, and your young men shall see visions, and your old men shall dream dreams"
(Acts 2:14-16 KJV).

Hence, according to Peter, those words spoken and heard through unknown tongues were fulfilling Joel's prophecies. Tongue is not anyone's native language. It can only be interpreted to the understanding of the people from different tribes.

Key Activation Prayers

Awesome Holy Spirit, come upon me and erase every burden of wrong beliefs about speaking in tongues and the usage of my natural tongue, now in Jesus' name. Amen!

Chapter

14

THE PURPOSE OF SPEAKING IN TONGUES IN THE LIFE OF A BELIEVER

CHAPTER FOURTEEN

THE PURPOSE OF SPEAKING IN TONGUES IN THE LIFE OF A BELIEVER

"For he that speaketh in an unknown tongue speaketh not unto men, but unto God:
for no man understandeth him; howbeit in the spirit he speaketh mysteries."
(1 Corinthians 14:2 KJV).

Praying in tongues has a lot of benefits. We will look into some of these benefits as we journey in this chapter. If speaking in tongues has no benefit, God would not have told us to desire it. Our opening text lets us know that it is a code for uttering mysteries. Who will not love to speak mysteries? Nobody! Let us begin to examine the benefits of speaking in tongues below:

1. Praying Out Mysteries in the Spirit
It is a great thing for one to be able to speak mysteries. What are mysteries? They are puzzles. They are things very difficult to understand and impossible to explain.
They are conundrums released in the form of breath. The only time one can speak like this is when one speaks in tongues. Speaking mysteries is only possible in the spirit.

"For he that speaketh in an unknown tongue speaketh not unto men, but unto God: for
no man understandeth him; howbeit in the spirit he speaketh mysteries"
(1 Corinthians 14:2 KJV).

Look at the description of what happened when the disciples began to speak in tongues:

"And they were all filled with the Holy Ghost, and began to speak with other tongues, as
the Spirit gave them utterance. And there were dwelling at Jerusalem Jews, devout men,
out of every nation under heaven. Now when this was noised abroad, the multitude came
together, and were confounded, because that every man heard them speak in his own
language. And they were all amazed and marvelled, saying one to another, Behold, are
not all these which speak Galilaeans? Cretes and Arabians, we do hear them speak in
our tongues the wonderful works of God"
(Acts 2:4-7, 11).

143

The Lord's disciples spoke mysteries. They never knew what they were saying. It was the angel of the Lord that began to interpret the tongues to the people. Those who gathered heard the tongues and were amazed. Everyone began to hear things about the kingdom of God and the wonderful works of God. When mysteries are interpreted, there is always light and understanding. A good example is what Paul said in the scripture below:

"Even the mystery which hath been hidden from ages and from generations, but now is made manifest to his saints: To whom God would make known what is the riches of the glory of this mystery among the Gentiles; which is Christ in you, the hope of glory" (Colossians 1:27 KJV).

We got to know the riches and depth of the glory of the "mystery" proclaimed in this scripture because it was interpreted by the writer "Paul" to be "Christ in us the hope of glory". However, it was hidden for ages until light and revelation came. Mysteries can be interpreted and that is the reason for the gift of interpretation of tongues. It is meant to interpret the mysteries of the unknown tongues. As you speak in tongues, you speak mysteries but desire to interpret mysteries.

2. *Speaking to God*
A good opportunity to speak to God directly in the Spirit is to speak in other tongues.

> *"For he that speaketh in an unknown tongue speaketh not unto men, but unto God*
> *(1 Corinthians 14:2a).*

Everyone has got so much to tell God. Sometimes, we are tired or lack words. When we pray in tongues, we speak to God directly.
The effect of praying to God directly is a quick answer. He who prays in other tongues quickly gets God's attention.

> *"And when they had prayed, the place was shaken where they were assembled together;*
> *and they were all filled with the Holy Ghost, and they spake the word of God with*
> *boldness" (Acts 4:31 KJV).*

3. *Spiritual Development and Edification*
A huge edification comes along with praying in tongues. Speaking in tongues is a building mechanism of the spirit. It causes improvement. It provokes instruction. Self-building takes place whenever one prays in tongues.

"But ye, beloved, building up yourselves on your most holy faith, praying in the Holy Ghost" (Jude 1:20).

This kind of self-building is from the demonstration of our most Holy faith which is "speaking in tongues".

"He that speaketh in an unknown tongue edifieth himself" (1 Corinthians 14:4a).

Edification means teaching, education, improvement, and building. However, speaking in tongues is a tool for spiritual development and improvement. If you want to grow faster in the spirit, pray in other tongues.

4. Receiving Might in the Inner Man

The best time to grow one's inner strength is to pray in tongues. When we wait on the Lord praying in the Holy Ghost, we renew strength. There are people who are easily discouraged due to the affairs of life. The best antidote to this form of weakness and all forms of spiritual weakness is praying in other tongues.

"He giveth power to the faint; and to them that have no might he increaseth strength. Even the youths shall faint and be weary, and the young men shall utterly fall: But they that wait upon the Lord shall renew their strength; they shall mount up with wings as eagles; they shall run, and not be weary; and they shall walk, and not faint" (Isaiah 40:29-31 KJV).

The Holy Ghost is a master in renewing our inner strength. When it comes to strength renewal, never joke with the Holy Ghost. The burnouts and the worn-outs can be repaired by the Holy Ghost when they pray in other tongues.

"That he would grant you, according to the riches of his glory, to be strengthened with might by his Spirit in the inner man" (Ephesians 3:16).
"Strengthened with all might, according to his glorious power, unto all patience and longsuffering with joyfulness" (Colossians 1:11 KJV).

5. Praying According to The Divine Will of God

There is so much joy when one knows he is praying according to the will of God. Speaking in other tongues helps one to press the right button in the spirit. That right button is the exact will of God required by man. A man may not know it, except it is revealed. Even if it is known, it might also be hard to carry out. This is the reason praying in other tongues is a weapon for driving the will of God.

> *"Likewise the Spirit also helpeth our infirmities: for we know not what we should pray for as we ought: but the Spirit itself maketh intercession for us with groanings which cannot be uttered. And he that searcheth the hearts knoweth what is the mind of the Spirit, because he maketh intercession for the saints according to the will of God"* *(Romans 8:26-27 KJV).*

6.   The Joint Account Prayer

The energy of the spirit is added to ours whenever we pray in the Spirit. Whether we are spiritually weak or physically strong, or vice versa, the Holy Spirit engages a joint prayer with us whenever we pray in tongues. Speaking in tongues is what licenses the Holy Spirit to join us in prayer. Whosoever engages in speaking in tongues literally permits the Spirit's aid in prayer.

> *"In the same way, the Spirit also joins to help in our weakness, because we do not know what to pray for as we should, but the Spirit Himself intercedes for us [a] with unspoken groanings"* *(Romans 8:26 HCSB).*

7.   Prompt response to the hunch of prayer burdens

There are burdens that may go beyond words. These burdens can be like a weight in the human spirit for days. No one may know what is exactly the issue or problem. However, by speaking in tongues, the spirit of man can speak the mysteries unto God, and a solution to the unknown is released in the Spirit.

> *"For if I pray in an unknown tongue, my spirit prayeth, but my understanding is unfruitful. What is it then? I will pray with the spirit, and I will pray with the understanding also: I will sing with the spirit, and I will sing with the understanding also"* *(1 Corinthians 14:14 KJV).*

8.   Divine Help

If you want to seek the divine help of God, or access God's divine help, speak in tongues.

"In the same way the Spirit also joins to help in our weakness, because we do not know what to pray for as we should, but the Spirit Himself intercedes for us with unspoken groanings" (Romans 8:26 HCSB).

Any kind of help is available in the Spirit for the believers. All that is needed is just to pray in other tongues and the solution will be birthed.

9.   Praying Amidst Is Avoided

Ignorance is one of the factors that make one pray amiss. Sometimes, if you don't pray in the Spirit, you might just pray amiss, asking selfishly. It is usually better to pray in the Spirit so as not to be a victim of the devil's plan and agenda. This is the way to conquer praying in vain. Praying in tongues helps one to pray the right way.

"Ye ask, and receive not, because ye ask amiss, that ye may consume it upon your lusts" (James 4:3).

10. *Subjecting The Body*

One of the ways to keep the body under subjection is to pray in other tongues. Praying in the Spirit breaks the longing of the flesh. It allows the Spirit to gain ascendancy in doing the will of God. Praying in the spirit tortures the will of the flesh *"Watch and pray, that ye enter not into temptation: the spirit indeed is willing, but the flesh is weak" (Mathew 26:41).*

"But I keep under my body, and bring it into subjection: lest that by any means, when I have preached to others, I myself should be a castaway" (1 Corinthians 9:27).

All forms of the lust of the flesh can be trashed in the place of prayer. When we pray in other tongues, personal lusts, people-sponsored lusts, and devil-initiated lusts can be destroyed.

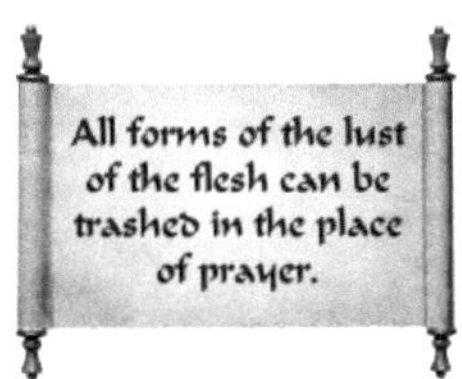

"Ye ask, and receive not, because ye ask amiss, that ye may consume it upon your lusts" (James 4:3).

11. *Exalting and Magnifying God in The Spirit*

Everyone who prays in tongue can mysteriously magnify God. Even if it was not planned, it can be done. In the place of speaking in tongues, it is possible to see God in a very big way. A window of vision can be opened for one to see the throne of God. So many spiritual openings of eyes do take place, thereby resulting in an unplanned magnification of our great God.

"And they of the circumcision which believed were astonished, as many as came with Peter, because that on the Gentiles also was poured out the gift of the Holy Ghost. For they heard them speak with tongues, and magnify God" (Acts 10:45-46).

12. Revelations

Many times, we can receive revelations in the place of praying in an unknown tongue. The Lord can open the eyes of the one praying to see things. Awareness can be turned on in the Spirit. A window of revelations can be opened by the immortal. One may be able to see beyond the visible into the realms of the Spirit. This is why praying in tongues is a powerful tool. This kind of prayer can enlighten the eyes of our spirit to know. It can provoke the spirit of wisdom and revelation in the knowledge of God.

"Cease not to give thanks for you, making mention of you in my prayers; That the God of our Lord Jesus Christ, the Father of glory, may give unto you the spirit of wisdom and revelation in the knowledge of him: The eyes of your understanding being enlightened; that ye may know what is the hope of his calling, and what the riches of the glory of his inheritance in the saints" (Ephesians 1:16-18).

13. Direction

The Apostles ministered to the Lord. Ministering to the Lord as used in this place means to do something of utmost spiritual meaning. It is bringing the highest form of service to God with the most holy faith. Several previous accounts have shown the Apostles' prayers and ministration unto the Lord. It was usually done by being filled with the Holy Ghost. In the middle of their fellowship, the Holy Ghost broke out with words of specific direction.

"Now there were in the church that was at Antioch certain prophets and teachers; as Barnabas, and Simeon that was called Niger, and Lucius of Cyrene, and Manaen, which had been brought up with Herod the tetrarch, and Saul. As they ministered to the Lord, and fasted, the Holy Ghost said, "Separate me Barnabas and Saul for the work whereunto I have called them. And when they had fasted and prayed, and laid their hands on them, they sent them away" (Acts 13:1-3 KJV).

This is usually possible whenever we commune in other tongues.

14. Deeper Communion with the Spirit of truth

Praying in tongues can open a bigger window of love, and sharing together with the Holy Spirit of truth. The people who have become acquainted with the Holy Spirit in the realm of the unknown tongues have mastered the appetite to love Him more.

"And I will pray the Father, and he shall give you another Comforter, that he may abide with you forever; Even the Spirit of truth; whom the world cannot receive, because it seeth him not, neither knoweth him: but ye know him; for he dwelleth with you, and shall be in you. I will not leave you comfortless: I will come to you" But the Comforter, which is the Holy Ghost, whom the Father will send in my name, he shall teach you all things, and bring all things to your remembrance, whatsoever I have said unto you"
(John 14:16-18, 26).

"The grace of the Lord Jesus Christ, and the love of God, and the communion of the Holy Ghost, be with you all. Amen" (2 Corinthians 13:14).
God wants love to increase in our hearts. He wants us to consistently be in fellowship with the Holy Spirit. He wants us to know Him more. The best way to usually turn on the light is to pray in the spirit more. This is why the Bible says
"And be not drunk with wine, wherein is excess; but be filled with the Spirit"
(Ephesians 5:18 KJV).

15. Singing Spiritual Songs "in the Spirit"

Have you ever desired to sing in the spirit? Have you ever imagined yourself singing mystery to God? You can always do that by speaking in an unknown tongue. The influence of the Holy Ghost upon the believers when speaking in unknown tongues can open up the scrolls of heavenly worship for participation in the spirit.

"Let the word of Christ dwell in you richly in all wisdom; teaching and admonishing one another in psalms and hymns and spiritual songs, singing with grace in your hearts to the Lord" (Colossians 3:16).

Singing spiritual songs causes grace to be multiplied in one's heart. The mystery-utterances at the place of singing spiritual songs are enough to cause mercy and grace to flow. This will lead me to tell the story of a young man who had the intuition to pray while He was walking along an express tarred road. He had the urge in his spirit but never knew what to pray about. He began to sing in the spirit, barely ten minutes later, a man's car skidded and hit a grass verge instead of hitting the man.

"And be not drunk with wine, wherein is excess; but be filled with the Spirit; Speaking to yourselves in psalms and hymns and spiritual songs, singing and making melody in your heart to the Lord" (Ephesians 5:18-19)

"What is it then? I will pray with the spirit, and I will pray with the understanding also: I will sing with the spirit, and I will sing with the understanding also" (1 Corinthians 14:15).

The ability to sing mystery in the Spirit comes with speaking in tongues and being filled with the Spirit. It opens up the realms where the right worship is engaged in collaboration with angels.

16. Persistent Infilling of the Spirit

One of the several ways to be filled with the Spirit is by speaking in tongues. If you want to get drunk in the Spirit quickly, get yourself into the arena of speaking in tongues. Suddenly, you will be filled with the Spirit. No one can restrain the power and the force of the Holy Ghost in such an atmosphere. Let me show you a few scriptures:

"And be not drunk with wine, wherein is excess; but be filled with the Spirit; Speaking to yourselves in psalms and hymns and spiritual songs, singing and making melody in your heart to the Lord" (Ephesians 5:18-19).

What was admonished in this scripture is "diverse speaking". The moment the dimension of speaking is opened, the revelation light is turned on, and one can mingle with the heavenly beings to sing in the unknown language unto God.

"And when they had prayed, the place was shaken where they were assembled together; and they were all filled with the Holy Ghost, and they spake the word of God with boldness" (Acts 4:31).

In this scenario, they prayed, of course, they prayed regularly in their most Holy faith as seen in other chapters of the Bible. The resultant effect of this is that they were filled with the Holy Ghost.

"And they were all filled with the Holy Ghost and began to speak with other tongues, as the Spirit gave them utterance" (Acts 2:4 KJV).

In this case, it was a first-time experience. They were filled and then they spoke in tongues. If one is in desire of a continuous infilling experience of the Holy Spirit, speaking in tongues can get you drunk quickly.

17. Rest and refreshing

The unknown tongue is a rest for the weary. When believers are weak not knowing what to pray for, and they open their tongues to pray in tongues, the Holy Ghost joins them to pray. He takes away their weakness. He gives them spiritual support in the place of prayers. This is a form of rest for the weary. It is a refreshing mechanism of the Spirit for getting the weak strengthened. If you seem to desire strength beyond weakness, just go ahead and pray in tongues.

"For with stammering lips and another tongue will he speak to this people. To whom he said, this is the rest wherewith ye may cause the weary to rest; and this is the refreshing: yet they would not hear" (Isaiah 28:11-12).

"Repent ye therefore, and be converted, that your sins may be blotted out, when the times of refreshing shall come from the presence of the Lord" (Acts 3:19).

18. Increase in Faith and Boldness

Speaking in tongues is a divine mechanism for inspiring faith, boldness, and confidence in the heart of the oppressed. The tormented usually catches a glimpse of light in the process of speaking in tongues.

"And when they had prayed, the place was shaken where they were assembled together; and they were all filled with the Holy Ghost, and they spake the word of God with boldness" (Acts 4:31).

19. Sharing of Love and Hope

One of the ways to get hope inspired in one's heart is by praying in tongues. When people lose hope because of daunting challenges, speaking in tongues can stir up new sparkles of hope and victory in their hearts. The best time to turn on the Holy Ghost's toggles for shedding His love abroad in our hearts is to pray. When one speaks in tongues, all of the love of the Father is reassured to the heart. When you are feeling discouraged, get up and pray. God's love will be re-echoed to your spirit, soul, and body.

"And hope maketh not ashamed; because the love of God is shed abroad in our hearts by the Holy Ghost which is given unto us" (Romans 5:5).

20. Affirming One's Refuge and Preservation

One can stir up the workings of the Spirit in the area of preservation by praying in tongues. Everyone who prays intensely in tongues usually experiences an assurance of the Spirit concerning refuge and preservation.

"He that dwelleth in the secret place of the most High shall abide under the shadow of the Almighty. I will say of the Lord, He is my refuge and my fortress: my God; in him will I trust. Surely he shall deliver thee from the snare of the fowler, and from the noisome pestilence" (Psalm 91:1-3 KJV).

"The Lord shall preserve thee from all evil: he shall preserve thy soul. The Lord shall preserve thy going out and thy coming in from this time forth, and even for evermore." (Psalm 121:7-8 KJV).

21. Stirring Up the Gifts of God

One of the many benefits of speaking in tongues is the ability to stir up the gifts of God. There are many dormant gifts of the spirit that can be activated as a result of speaking in tongues. The Spirit of God can help one to pray in that direction, bringing inactive gifts of the spirit to the limelight.

"Wherefore I put thee in remembrance that thou stir up the gift of God, which is in thee by the putting on of my hands" (2 Timothy 1:6).

22. Bringing Fast Tongue And Fast Feet Under Subjection

There are some tongues and feet that are too quick in operation. The tongues talk in an unruly manner, while the feet make too much haste. Speaking in tongues is part of the antidotes to this problem.

"But the tongue can no man tame; it is an unruly evil, full of deadly poison "(James 3:8).

"These six things doth the Lord hate: yea, seven are an abomination unto him:
A proud look, a lying tongue, and hands that shed innocent blood, An heart that deviseth
wicked imaginations, feet that be swift in running to mischief"
(Proverb 6:16-18 KJV).

23. Engaging The Promise Of God

The best time to engage God's promises is to pray in the Spirit. When you pray in tongues with the scriptures in your mouths, you are giving the promises of God the wings to fly.

"And when they had prayed, the place was shaken where they were assembled together;
and they were all filled with the Holy Ghost, and they spake the word of God with
boldness" (Acts 4:31).

24. Travailing For Urgent Delivery

There is a laborious dimension of speaking in tongues that can be engaged in the place of prayers. This dimension can help someone to get results quickly. It can bring about sudden changes and transformations on every side. It can cause one to deliver greatness and give birth to any desired changes. This dimension is called "travailing".

"Who hath heard such a thing? who hath seen such things? Shall the earth be made to
bring forth in one day? or shall a nation be born at once? for as soon as Zion travailed,
she brought forth her children" (Isaiah 66:8)

"My little children, of whom I travail in birth again until Christ be formed in you"
(Galatians 4:19).

25. Revival of The Spirit

Praying in tongues is an instrument for promoting revival in the spirit. Everyone who has got the most lasting revivals at one point went through a season of intense prayer that opened up the portals for revival. It is impossible for the spirit of a man to die-out and burn-out where there is an intense fire of prayer. Revival in the spirit goes beyond strength but constant engagement and renewal.

"For which cause we faint not; but though our outward man perish, yet the inward man
is renewed day by day" (2 Cor. 4:16).

"Hast thou not known? hast thou not heard, that the everlasting God, the Lord, the Creator of the ends of the earth, fainteth not, neither is weary? there is no searching of his understanding. He giveth power to the faint; and to them that have no might he increaseth strength. Even the youths shall faint and be weary, and the young men shall utterly fall" (Isaiah 40:28-31).

26. Supplication for All Saints

It is possible to make intercession for all saints by speaking in an unknown tongue. There are times when speaking in tongues engenders someone to make intercessions for other people. Those who are yielded to the spirit are usually victims of this. They find themselves praying fervidly in the spirit, and asking something earnestly on behalf of someone.

"Praying always with all prayer and supplication in the Spirit, and watching there unto with all perseverance and supplication for all saints"
(Ephesians 6:18).

Key Activation Prayers

Awesome Holy Spirit, fulfil the purpose of speaking in tongues in my life. Let all the benefits be fulfilled in my life and personal walk with you in Jesus' name. Amen!